SUICIDE
THE SIGNS AND SOLUTIONS

FINLEY H. SIZEMORE

VICTOR BOOKS®
A DIVISION OF SCRIPTURE PRESS PUBLICATIONS INC.
USA CANADA ENGLAND

Scripture quotations are from the *King James Version*.
Recommended Dewey Decimal Classification: 362.22
Suggested Subject Heading: SUICIDE—PREVENTION

Library of Congress Catalog Card Number: 87-62483
ISBN: 0-89693-425-X

© 1988 by SP Publications, Inc.

▰▰▰▰ CONTENTS

Man has only one life. This life can be taken from him but cannot be given back if taken. It is his but cannot be given away. It is his to live, but only once; it cannot be lived over again. He can destroy his earthly life but cannot end his existence. Yet while living their lives, millions suffer the pangs of psychological, social, physical, and spiritual pain. The pain is so intense that they seek to end their lives by suicide. Still there is help for these people; the church has an opportunity and responsibility to serve as the vehicle for giving this help. This longtime conviction gave birth to this book, a volume intended to give encouragement and guidance to those desiring to help suicidal people.

Early chapters deal with theoretical matters, such as the scope and intensity of suicide and understanding suicide. Latter chapters address practical concerns, including how to keep a person from killing himself and putting the suicide epidemic in true perspective as a church mission of hope for those who want out of life.

This book is not written within any one frame of reference. Several areas of study have been drawn upon, but mainly psychology and theology. The book is more the creative work of a Christian with formal training in both psychology and theology. Suicidal people with whom I have walked as they sought to cope with despair have enriched and expanded this formal training. Interaction with relatives and friends of suicide victims, who were left with confusion, grief, and many times guilt feelings, has also influenced the author.

Several illustrations are suppositional cases based on clinical experience. I am especially indebted to the people who granted permission for a part of their struggle to be used. For the main concern of this work is not to speak about theology or psychology, but rather to communicate to the needs of people whose lives will be touched by suicide. A result is the possibility that some of the contents of the book will not be acceptable to all readers. The possibility is increased by my acceptance of the Bible as the inspired Word of God. I am well aware of opposite views in psychology and even in theology. If the book is found useful by those who seek to help people who are caught in a suicide struggle, it will serve the purpose for which it was written.

1 THE SUICIDE EPIDEMIC: "STOP MY WORLD! I WANT TO GET OFF!"

Excitement burst from every direction that evening at the state fair. While bright lights flickered across the faces of fun-loving people, stimulating music sounded through the fairgrounds. Children and the young in heart moved from ride to ride, talking and laughing with merriment; everybody was enjoying the fun—that is, almost everybody.

Suddenly, screams pierced through the night. Eyes turned toward the merry-go-round, where a frightened little girl was crying, begging, "Stop, stop, I want to get off! I hate this terrible ride."

The cry of the little girl is the cry of hundreds of Americans. The ride of life is more than they can handle; they cannot cope with their world and want to get off life's merry-go-round. In panic they cry out, many times unheard, "Stop my world; let me off—I can't endure this frightening existence!"

These people are not afraid of nonexistence; they are afraid of existence. The problem for them is *being*, not nonbeing. Therefore, many people do not want an endless life; consequently, their resistance to life often results in self-defeating or self-destructive behavior.

Human resistance to endless existence emerges in many areas of thought and behavior. For example, consider the theological doctrine called human annihilation that rejects the continuity of life after death. Buddhism, another example, propagates the belief and practice of extinction of desire and self-awareness, adherents thereby becoming oblivious to conscious existence and external reality.

All of us, to some degree, seek to ease the awareness of a separate and permanent existence by daydreaming or retreating into a make-believe world, perhaps by reading a novel or watching a TV drama. Some daydreaming is natural and can be useful when limited. It can release tension when we face an unbearable and unchangeable situation. Pleasant experiences of the past can be recaptured to give present enjoyment. Daydreaming can compensate for real or imagined inferiorities. When it has the element of planning and creative thinking, it can become tomorrow's achievement. Granted, it can be useful and healthy, but "building castles in the air" and none on the ground is wasting energy and moving away from the challenge of a separate and permanent life. "Forever blowing bubbles" that have no effect on reality, to deaden reality, is a reaction to a fear of life.

Such responses as these often defeat or cheat us, but the most pathetic response to the fear of life is suicide. Self-murder is one of the greatest problems facing our society. Once only a drop in the American population bucket, suicide has now filled the bucket, and is spilling over to become a national concern. It is a problem for the person who has suicidal tendencies; it is a problem for the family of the person who attempts or commits suicide; it is a problem for a caring church.

Suicide is problem enough to be the eighth leading cause of death in the United States. The suicide rate among young people alone has doubled in a generation. Every time the clock ticks off a minute, at least one person in our country attempts to die by self-destruction; a sad fact is that many of these attempts are successful. In 1984, 29,060 people in our country killed themselves. According to this figure over 550 Americans end their lives every week (*Monthly Vital Statistics Report*. Vol. 33, Sept. 26, 1985).

SUICIDE AND TEENAGERS

The fear of one mother was very clear in her words: "I don't want something to happen to my child. How can I know when there is a danger? Somebody should do something to stop this senseless self-murder of teenagers." The fear of this mother is multiplied over and over in mothers and fathers throughout America. Parents of emotionally troubled teenagers, especially, worry about their children.

Some of these frantic parents are so concerned that nightmares disturb their sleep. And they become more frantic as they learn that the teenage suicide is an even greater problem than reports indicate, for they find that many teenage suicides are reported as accidents to protect the reputations of victims and the feelings of survivors. They learn that the self-murder rate for "older teens has tripled since the 1950s, making suicide the second cause of death (after accidents) among adolescents in the United States" ("Prevention," *Glamour*, April 1985). Parents sense the frustration of psychologists, social workers, counselors, school personnel, and police in seeking an explanation for the suicide epidemic among teenagers.

When parents read reports that one teenage suicide tragedy strikes every 90 minutes in the United States, they have reason for alarm. Faced with pornography, divorce, drugs, crime, abortion, and similar problems, many teenagers are losing all hope. Suicide is the third-leading cause of teen deaths, and the second-leading cause among college students, according to newly released statistics. While the suicide rate for the rest of the population remained stable, the rate for ages 15-24 rose by 41 percent between 1970 and 1978. By 1983, 12 out of 100,000 in that age group had committed suicide.

Parents ask: "Could suicide happen in our family? Could we find our child hanging from a rope, dead from a gunshot, or lifeless from carbon-monoxide poisoning?" Knowing about the normal struggles of teenagers during adolescence, they know that one suicide could ignite others. Aware of peer pressure and teenage confusion, they know the danger for troubled youth.

News articles such as one on the popular Japanese singer Yukiko Okada, who killed herself and set off a wave of teen suicide, emphasize that teen suicide is contagious:

A 12-year-old girl jumped to her death today from a suburban high-rise, becoming the 33rd Japanese youth to commit suicide since a popular teenage singer killed herself two and one half weeks ago, authorities said.

Few notes left behind by young suicide victims directly referred to the death of the singer Yukiko Okada on

April 8, but her death and the publicity surrounding it are believed responsible in part for the rash of suicides in a country where suicide by young people is a long-standing problem.

Twenty-one of the thirty-three youths who have killed themselves since Miss Okada threw herself from a Tokyo office building also jumped to their deaths from buildings. Others ended their lives by hanging themselves, setting themselves on fire, or asphyxiation (*Aiken [S.C.] Standard*, April 24, 1986).

Alert parents accept there are suicide risks for distraught teens; consequently, they are afraid their child will join the approximately 6,000 young people who kill themselves each year.

Published reports of teenage suicide keep many parents on edge:

■ Seven young people at Bryan High School on the outskirts of Omaha, Nebraska attempted to die by self-murder within a period of five days. Three of them—a girl, sixteen; a boy, fifteen; and a boy, eighteen—ended their earthly existence. These teens were average teenagers like the ones living in our homes, worshiping in our churches, and attending our schools. That is, people who knew them suspected no outstanding emotional problems.

■ Tragedy occurred in New York's Westchester and Putnam Counties when five boys committed suicide during February 1984. Four of these boys used the same method for ending their lives—hanging.

The loss and hurt of teenage suicide is indeed real. It is tragedy beyond repair; the loss of what could have been is a tragic cost to their friends, their families, and their communities.

Many parents and concerned leaders see the classroom as doing more to encourage suicide than to discourage it.

Four years ago, after listening to a discussion of suicide methods in his Perry, Florida classroom, Gale Dickert's 16-year-old son went home and drowned himself.

In Richmond, Virginia the same year, Patricia Pulling's son took his life to escape a role he was assigned in a classroom fantasy game.

According to *Insight* magazine (Nov. 17, 1986), the Pulling youth committed suicide when he became too involved with his role in "Dungeons and Dragons," an elaborate role-playing game being enacted in his class for gifted and talented students. He received an order to "plunder, pillage, and destroy." Rather than harm others, he chose to kill himself, says his mother.

"Suicide . . . is a moral issue," his mother says. "Suicide is difficult to talk about without the subject of an afterlife coming up. If schools can't talk about religion, if a teacher doesn't have values the family holds, you can get into some real problems."

Phyllis Schlafly, founder of the Eagle Forum profamily group, is an outspoken opponent of legislation and school programs on suicide prevention, the *Insight* article continued.

"The worst thing children can do is sit around in the classroom and discuss suicide," she says. "It's very likely that whatever is done will be worse than nothing at all.

"Courses in school are extremely damaging and very likely cause suicides in the same way the TV documentaries cause them. I'm sure the people connected with them had good intentions, but they caused suicides."

To emphasize her point, she cites the fact that some suicide prevention education is woven into courses on death and dying, in some of which children are even asked to write their own wills and epitaphs.

You may say: "Why be so concerned about a few hundred teens who kill themselves? They are only a small percentage of the teenage population." Granted, teen suicides compared with teens who choose life instead of death, represent only a small percentage of the teen population. Nevertheless, when we accept that they are living souls, not things, their loss appears in a different light. When we note that teenage suicide is the second leading cause of death, the percentage becomes alarming.

Even one teenage suicide is a tragedy, for self-murder is more than a percentage: it is the loss of a person. When we sense the pain and loss to the loved ones and friends of the victims, the percentage is a tragedy. When the senseless act of suicide strikes close to home, the percentage is frightening. If the teenage self-murder is a friend, a neighbor, or a family member, the percentage rips our hearts apart. Yes, only a relatively few teenagers kill themselves every year, but the suicide percentage means young lives are snuffed out; the pain is horribly real.

A young man walked out into quicksand on the coast of a Southern state. It appeared so inviting to a young fellow seeking adventure, but suddenly he realized that he was in serious trouble. Slowly he was sinking down into the sand as the ground gave way under his feet; the more he struggled, the more he sank. Becoming frantic with fear, he cried out to his friend who was a few hundred feet away: "Help, I am sinking."

When his friend saw his predicament, he had to make a hasty decision. Being a native of the area, he knew that the quicksand meant possible death. Therefore, he concluded that he had three choices: he could assume a morbid outlook on the situation and see it as hopeless, thereby doing nothing; he could rush in to help his friend and sink with him into the quicksand; or, he could in some way reach out to help and rescue his friend.

He quickly made the third choice. He rushed to a nearby boat dock, grabbed a rope, and threw one end of it to the young man. Though it was a real struggle, the sinking man was able to use the rope to free himself from the quicksand. This young man continued to live because someone cared and rescued him from his predicament.

Teenagers are sinking in the quicksands of life. We who care, like the friend of the sinking young man, must quickly make a choice. We can become morbid in our outlook and view the epidemic as hopeless; we can rush into the quicksand and become submerged in the suicidal despair; or, we can make a sensible approach to the problem and attempt to rescue the victims of this dangerous and deadly epidemic. Certainly, it isn't a simple matter, but there is light at the end of the tunnel. We must not be paralyzed by statistics; we must seek a solution to the problem.

SUICIDE AND THE ECONOMICALLY DEPRESSED

Though the major focus in the media is on teenage suicide, self-murder snuffs out the lives of thousands of people of all ages, especially when they face depressing situations. In a Midwestern city, a sixty-year-old man, active in an evangelical church, lost job after job. Finally, facing the loss of his home because an investment didn't pay off, he shocked the church and community by shooting himself.

The plight of economically depressed farmers has received widespread publicity. Millions were horrified at news involving an Iowa farmer. With his bank about to foreclose on his mortgage, he killed the bank president, a fellow farmer, his own wife, and then took his own life.

Other farmers have given up on life under similar circumstances. High prices for needed farm equipment and supplies, often along with crop failures and low prices for produce, have sent thousands of farmers to banks to borrow funds. Then unable to meet mortgage payments, they see the fruits of their labors vanishing. Having spent years of hard work, they know that it will be only a matter of time before they will be completely out of business. Often their farms were handed down by parents and grandparents, and it's more than many farmers can handle.

The loss of the family farm, and along with it the loss of community standing, triggers suicide for some farmers. The suicide note left by the Iowa farmer speaks despair for himself, and the despair felt by many other farmers. His note expressed that he could no longer handle his problems; he could not cope with life.

However, not only farmers but many other adults and young people turn to suicide because of the economic squeeze. The much publicized case of Johnnie Holley's family shows the spread of the suicide epidemic because of financial problems (*Newsweek*, September 10, 1984). His son killed himself so there would be one fewer to feed. Thus financial difficulties trigger this painful epidemic with people on many levels of American life.

Whether the loss is a farm, a family income, or some other financial loss, it triggers suicide in some people. The victims are unable to cope with the loss; life becomes unbearable. While suicide because of economic stress may be regarded of little general consequences, a caring person must ask: "What would happen to countless individuals in a nationwide economic depression?"

SUICIDE AND ALCOHOLICS

While several drunks sat in a local bar doing their usual nightly thing—drinking—one man became very depressed and talked about ending his life. Another man told him: "Don't talk about killing yourself; the Bible says that a person should not commit suicide."

"Oh yeah," responded a third drunk; "what do you know about the Bible?"

The first man replied: "I know about the Bible; I can quote all the Lord's Prayer."

"I bet you ten dollars you can't," said the other drunk.

So the bet was on as both drunks handed their ten dollars to the depressed drunk for him to hold during the betting. It was now time for the first drunk to prove his knowledge of the Bible by quoting the Lord's Prayer. He quoted: "Now I lay me down to sleep; I pray the Lord my soul to keep. If I should die before I wake, I pray the Lord my soul to take." The second drunk said: "He does know it; give him the twenty dollars." But the depressed drunk was no place to be seen; he had left with the twenty dollars; it had helped him over his depression.

The suicide rate is high among alcoholics; and, dollars alone won't cure it. Workers in the field of alcoholic treatment know that suicide among alcoholics is inevitable for many. Estimates indicate that suicide in the alcoholic population is approximately 30 percent higher than the national suicide average. In view of the constant increase in the alcoholic population, suicide will continue to increase among alcoholics.

Perhaps someone will say: "He is only an alcoholic; why be alarmed?" True, the alcoholic who kills himself is only an alcoholic, but he is some mother's son. He is a living soul, a creature of God. Even though a miserable existence, his life is precious. Why should it end in senseless self-murder?

SUICIDE AND THE ELDERLY

Grandfather and granddaughter were taking their weekly walk in the city park, talking as they strolled along that Sunday afternoon. Usually, on their walk, the little granddaughter told grandfather about her experiences at school the past week, and asked him questions about her Sunday School lesson for that morning. Their walk in the park was a wonderful experience for both grandfather and granddaughter.

As the Sunday School lesson for this Sunday was about Noah and the Flood, the little girl was bubbling over with information about it. Finally, she asked, "Grandfather, were you and grandmother on the ark?" He replied, "No, honey, we were not on the ark." She then exclaimed, "How did you keep from getting drowned in the Flood?"

Growing old is a rich experience for many people; but, for a few people, old age with its additional coping problems is more than they can handle. These people are overcome with life and turn to suicide. While old age can be beautiful, it can also be, for some, unbearable.

We must consider suicide among the elderly of our nation a significant part of the suicide epidemic. A few years ago, an expert in gerontology, Dr. Robert Butler, estimated that perhaps "25 percent of all suicides are committed by persons over 65" (*U.S. News and World Report*, July 2, 1982, p. 51). Many older persons are not able to cope with affliction, boredom, or isolation; consequently, they give up life's struggle to die by their own hands. Since people are living longer, the suicide epidemic among the elderly will likely increase.

Many people consider this statistic to have little personal significance. Younger people may shrug and say, "This would never happen to my parents or grandparents," while others would simply have little interest in what happens to their parents or grandparents. If the reader falls into the first group of people, don't be so sure it won't happen to one of your loved ones. If you fall into the second group, remember, you may someday be old. If you do live to be old, and cannot cope with life, the statistic will have meaning for you then; in fact, you could become a statistic—a suicide victim.

SUICIDE AND PRISONERS

We must not overlook prisoners, another high risk group in the suicide epidemic, in considering the spreading of self-murder. When we hear of one prisoner hanging himself, we do not think of jail suicide as a big problem. However, when we make a table of jail suicides throughout the nation, we find that it is a significant part of our suicide epidemic. The *Washington Post* reported that jail suicides are alarming, quoting a national law enforcement official as viewing the "sharp increase" in jail suicides as a national disgrace ("Jail Inmates' Suicide Rate Rises Sharply," *Washington Post*, February 18, 1985).

Again, the reader may say: "No big deal, he is only a jailbird." Yes, he is only a jailbird, but he is a human being, somebody. A mother once endured the pains of childbirth to bring him into the world. A father once looked down on his little chubby face and said, "My son!" The prisoner is a living soul and God loves him. Jesus Christ died on the cross for him. He is only a jailbird, a jailbird with a problem; still, it is wrong for him to take his life. As with the other high-risk groups, the jail population will continue to increase, and along with it jail suicides. Yes, such senseless loss of life is a national disgrace.

SUICIDE TOUCHES EVERY LEVEL OF LIFE

One day Peter, an active four-year-old boy, became frightened while playing by himself some distance from his house. He suddenly looked down and saw his shadow. Never having focused on his shadow before, he thought that it was a ghost, for he had heard about ghosts. Terrified, Peter started running to get away from this unknown thing that was following him. But this thing of terror stayed with him; the faster Peter ran, the faster his shadow ran, for obviously a person cannot outrun his shadow. Only after his mother talked with him did his fears subside.

Like Peter, people in the suicide epidemic are frightened of their own shadows—themselves. Though intelligent and well bred, we are generally a people on the run. We are trying to run away from a reflection of our own lives, but such escape is impossible. Sometimes, like the frightened boy, we do not recognize ourselves. Anyway, as we American citizens try to escape our lives, we push suicide statistics higher and higher. Nevertheless, where there is a shadow, there is light somewhere to cast the shadow. This light is our ray of hope; therefore, even in this suicide epidemic, we know there is hope for the hopeless.

Regardless of the high risk group we consider when viewing the suicide epidemic, the statistics are alarming. If we accept that every human being has the potential for abundant life, we have to be shocked at suicide's waste. The suicide epidemic sweeping across our country distresses us; the sorrow signal of suicide despair alarms us; we care about those who are dying from self-inflicted wounds. We are bothered by the people who die from an overdose of pills, a jump from a bridge, or from automobile exhaust fumes. We are alarmed when people hang themselves, shoot themselves, or destroy their lives by some other absurd act.

We may feel that we are exempt from this problem, especially if we are church people. Such a feeling is not realistic, because suicide touches the lives of people on every level, Christians included. The attempt or suicide of a family member, a friend, or acquaintance has touched most of us. Almost all of us have had, at sometime in life, a thought about suicide. I am not suggesting that every person considers killing himself. We do, though, live with the raw material of human existence; and we are aware of our separate existence enough to realize that life is more than we can handle alone.

SUICIDE CONCERNS THE CHURCH

A wealthy teenage girl owned a valuable race horse that one day appeared to be sick. So the girl phoned a veterinarian, who assured her, after examining the patient, that it was not really sick. But since the horse was sluggish, the vet explained, he would give the animal an energy shot. To the owner's surprise, the energy shot got immediate results; the horse broke loose and dashed down the highway at an excessive speed. In his excitement the veterinarian started explaining to the girl what he gave the horse. She screamed, "Never mind what you gave him; just give me a double dose; I have to catch that horse!"

The suicide crisis is moving at an excessive rate of speed. We, like the horse owner, don't need explanations as much as we need a double dose of energy power to catch it. As life has become more complicated, suicide has changed from a few scattered cases to a deluge of cases. It is a problem that is sweeping through every city and community, touching many who have become involved in some way with a church.

Because God expects us to have a special love for people, we as Christians should be concerned for suicidal people. We must be alert to those people who may be struggling with ideas of self-harm and need special attention. We should have deep concern about this problem that is overwhelming our Christian brothers and sisters—and nonbelievers alike. Our leaders—pastors, youth workers, music directors, educational directors, ushers, deacons, Sunday School teachers—must be alert to the needs generated by the suicide epidemic, and accept those with suicidal tendencies as part of our Christian mission.

Is it possible that many of us have blind spots which blot out the reality of this suicide epidemic? A pastor is not able to see the storms that rage in the lives of people who listen to him preach. A person sitting in a Sunday School class could be thinking about killing himself or herself. A young person in youth activities could be dead from self-inflicted wounds before the next activity. A choir member who sings every Sunday in a church choir could be crying inside while making joyful sounds with his lips. The person who is ushered to a seat for a Sunday morning worship service could be rolled down the aisle for a suicide funeral service before the next Sunday morning.

This headline appeared in October 1987 in the weekly paper of a prominent Christian college: "Suicide Concern Rises on Campus." The article went on to say that a freshman and an upper-classman had attempted suicide at the beginning of the school year. Some ten students attempt suicide at that college annually, with September and February typically being the "bad months."

People across our land are killing themselves in staggering numbers. Many of them are members or adherents of our churches. Churches must wake up to the need: time is flying; Satan is lying; people are dying! What can the church do?

LIGHT AT THE END OF THE TUNNEL

This book can help you four ways: (1) It will help you understand the suicide struggle of those who choose death rather than life; (2) provide information for training people in the identification, evaluation, and liberation of persons enslaved by thoughts of suicide; (3) give you information that you can use to motivate others toward a practical concern for suicidal people; and (4) offer a missionary challenge to the church itself.

2 THE NEED TO UNDERSTAND SUICIDE

The conference was unusual in the fullest sense of the word. At the invitation of the President of the United States, experts from every state had come to Washington, D.C. to help find an answer to the suicide epidemic. The President opened the conference by saying: "America must turn her resources to finding a solution to suicide." In response, the experts gave loud and long applause to his opening remark; for they too had very strong feelings about getting help for people struggling with suicide. All the participants of the conference expected that it would turn the suicide tide and curb the epidemic.

When the applause subsided, the President continued: "You who desire to do so will be given an opportunity to share your theory of the cause and cure of suicide. You will have one minute; so be brief and clear in your presentation. When your name is called, if you care to contribute, please speak into one of the microphones near you."

One by one several of the experts stepped to a microphone and gave an opinion of the cause of suicide, and then prescribed a cure for it. The first expert stated: "Mr. President, suicide is caused by a chemical imbalance; therefore I propose that millions of dollars be allocated to find a drug that will cure it." Another expert stated: "Mr. President, drug abuse causes most suicides; thus I suggest that the millions of dollars be spent to stop the flow of illicit drugs now flowing into our country." The next speaker stated: "Mr. President, suicide is caused by mental illness; I recommend that the millions of dollars be spent to treat mentally ill people, and thereby cure the suicide epidemic." Still another speaker advocated: "Mr. President, much suicide is caused by publicity about suicide; I prefer that we use any money to eliminate publicity about suicide."

Eventually, after several other theories of the cause and cure of suicide had been expressed, the last speaker said: "Mr. President, I respect the opinions of these men and women; they are well qualified to help solve the suicide epidemic; however, they are wrong about the cause and the cure. Personal sin causes all suicide; so let us use the millions of dollars to get people to stop sinning."

The President dropped his head for a moment, and then said: "Ladies and gentlemen, this conference makes me very confused. If we cannot agree on the cause of suicide, how can we find a cure? Evidently, we do not understand suicide; consequently, there is no need to continue the conference. Thank you for coming to Washington; have an enjoyable and safe trip back to your homes."

No, there has not been a news blackout; there has not been any such conference in Washington, D.C. I presented this report of a suppositional conference to emphasize that there are many different opinions about suicide among experts. If the President were to hold such a conference, much confusion would likely result from it.

Nevertheless, this would not mean that all the theories are false. On the contrary, many of the theories would have some truth in them. Much of the confusion about the suicide epidemic is caused by exclusive opinions which see only one cause, and fail to acknowledge different levels of cause and effect. Also, much confusion results from the emphasis put on causes and problems rather than on troubled people. Any cause or problem of suicide is a part of human functioning.

For convenience in our discussion of people's understanding of suicide, we will arbitrarily divide the population of the United States into four categories. First, there are the many untouched citizens, who give little thought to the problem of suicide and therefore have little or no understanding of the matter. They have never become directly involved with it; they themselves do not have suicidal tendencies and no member of their family has killed himself. As a result, they say: "Suicide is not my problem."

If you are in this category, you are not protected from this problem. Past exemption from involvement with suicide does not guarantee future protection from it. When we consider suicide statistics, we know that life can change for any one of us; that which has not happened in the past could well happen in the future.

The second group consists of individuals who also have little understanding of suicide, and intensify the problem by relating to suicidal people in a manner which undermines their coping abilities. This category of people inflict hurt, many times by words and actions, driving a friend or loved one to death.

The third category consists of citizens who know about suicide because the life or death of a suicidal person has touched their lives. They have learned about suicide the hard way and have emotional scars to attest to the seriousness of the problem. People in this grouping became suddenly involved with suicide. A relative, a neighbor, or friend either attempted to kill himself or did kill himself. From their experience with this tragedy, individuals in category three have learned firsthand of its pain; they have been through the suicide trauma; it has left them with unanswered questions and unspeakable grief.

The fourth category contains people who themselves are suicidal; they feel the pain of despair but do not necessarily understand suicide. People in this division reside somewhere on the suicide range—from weak annoying thoughts of suicide to maximum despair. Their place on this suicide range determines their mental and emotional pain; because the closer they get to the fatal act, the more misery they feel. Due to their miserable feeling, the thinking of people in this category often becomes extremely confused.

Many people recognize suicide as being a real problem; they care about suicidal people, and want to help. But they do not always understand suicide or know how to help. Others know or care little, if any, about the suicide problem. Regardless of people's attitude toward self-murder, they have formed beliefs about it. And many people have erroneous, and sometimes dangerous beliefs about this subject.

Almost all people admit that suicide is a tough problem

for the human race to understand; therefore any discussion of this topic should examine the question: "Do people understand suicide?"

Scripture records the agonizing cry of several people while they were in a suicide crisis. From four of these people we can learn some interesting facts about suicide and see the difference between suicide facts and the suicide myths considered in the last part of this chapter.

A SUICIDE PICTURE OUT OF FOCUS

Moses, a great servant of the Lord, reached a moment of despair by feeling that the load of life was too heavy for him to endure (Num. 11:11-15). While he faced this impossible situation, he told the Lord that it would be a kindness if He would kill him right that moment. Consider the following truths about suicide that relate to Moses' despair:

■ *Even a great spiritual leader may be overcome by the burdens of life to see no way out other than suicide (v. 15).* Moses was a great leader, but he found himself in an awkward position because of the burden of all the disgruntled people. As he led his people from Egypt to Canaan, they became disagreeable and grumbled about their present situation and wanted to return to Egypt. During this time of trouble Moses experienced distorted vision and sank in despair.

Even though he realized that his task was too big for any human to handle alone, he was committed to it. He saw no way out of the situation; therefore, in his distress he preferred death to the burden of all the unhappy people. Moses let his burdens hide the resources of God. And, he let his own feelings blind him to the talent of other people in the group.

■ *Moses was infected with the despondent spirit of the disgruntled people (vv. 11-15).* One confusing aspect of suicide is the way one suicide sets off other suicides. This is illustrated by the cluster of suicides among teenagers. Even though Moses did not become suicidal because of the disgruntled people, their despondency did ignite despondency in him. Despair is sometimes contagious.

Perhaps someone will ask: "If Moses had killed himself, would his suicide have set off suicides among the Israelites?" This is an interesting question; however, we cannot give a direct answer to it because of our lack of information. We know much about Moses' suicide crisis; yet there are details that we do not know. Based on some present-day outbreaks of suicide because of the suicide of one person, we can speculate that an outbreak would have been a possibility. The morbid spirit of the disgruntled Israelites would have been fertile ground for a suicide epidemic.

■ *While in suicidal despair, Moses was submerged in self-pity (vv. 11-14).* He felt so sorry for himself that he could not see God's blessings. Since the days of Moses, many of God's children have let their ordeals blot out their blessings. Self-pity prevents them from seeing that every life has blessings in it as well as burdens. As it is easy for trouble to hide the good things in a person's life, pain may blind one to plenty; fighting with one's enemies may hide one's friends; one's poverty may hide one's health. When trouble threw Moses' life off course, his blessings became obscure; he could not see beyond his own afflictions.

Usually, people who suffer from self-pity find themselves cut off from the good things of life and their troubles multiply.

■ *Moses wanted to die to escape the total failure of his hopes and efforts (vv. 13-14).* He felt that his hopes of leading the Israelites to the Promised Land had been dashed. The people had rejected his leadership, leaving him in suicidal despair. Most people, like Moses, find it hard in dealing with failure. He had really put himself into his work, trying to get the Israelites to the Promised Land; now he felt his work was useless. He had high hopes for the people; now he felt hopeless. Faced with failure, Moses wanted to escape his life.

■ *God does not always listen to the foolish praying of despondent Christians (v. 15).* Suppose that the Lord had answered Moses' prayer. God could have raised up another leader for His people and let Moses die in his despair; however, this is not the Lord's way of handling a Christian in despair.

Rather, God offers life rather than death to a suicidal person: God offered Moses a way out of his burdens and despair; He gave Moses nearly forty years of productive living; He showed him the blessings of life as well as the blights of life. A suicidal child of God overcame his troubles to make a significant impact on history, and acquire a permanent place in eternity. God wants life for us, not death.

A WILDERNESS SCHOOL FOR A DISCOURAGED PROPHET

Elijah, who made an impact on people in low and high places, went into the wilderness, sat down under a tree, and told the Lord he had enough of life (1 Kings 19:3-4). He said, in effect, "Lord, I've got to die sometime, and it might as well be now."

From Elijah's story we see how discouragement saps the vitality out of life and moves one to thoughts of death. Elijah in God's power performed miracles; he had been doing big things for God. Now he felt that only he was left, the last "Christian" on earth; consequently, he withdrew from the struggle. Out alone in the wilderness under a broom tree, Elijah wanted to call it quits; he was overcome with discouragement. What did Elijah learn from this experience? At least five important lessons that are also important for us.

1. *Elijah learned to tune his ears to the voice of God (vv. 11-13).* When a troubled child of God is overcome by discouragement, wanting to die to escape life, he must learn where and how God is speaking. Elijah had programmed himself to look for God in earth-shaking events, or stormy encounters. He had failed to listen to the still small voice speaking to his heart to teach him that things are sometimes different from their appearance. One should not limit the work of the Lord to sensational events; a troubled Christian makes a mistake when he sits in despair looking for a miracle. God does not answer all of one's troubles with outstanding or sensational miracles.

2. *Elijah learned the misery of a displaced child of God (vv. 9-10).* When a troubled Christian lets discouragement take him out of the Lord's service, his life is out of spiritual bounds. God had plans for His people; Elijah had a significant place in those plans. God had scheduled Elijah for action; discouragement took him out of action.

Elijah, a troubled child of God, had a choice; he could sit in discouragement, or he could fill his place in God's work.

This dynamic prophet learned that he was in the wrong place, because he was out of place. Because he was in the wrong place, sitting on the sidelines of life in discouragement, he was miserable, wanting to die to get away from his misery.

3. *Elijah learned that he had made an F in math (vv. 14-18).* Elijah discovered that discouragement often impairs judgment; his self-pity had short-circuited his mental calculator. When he computed the religious scene to see who stood for the Lord, he arrived at zero. A person in a downcast spirit should not attempt spiritual assessments. Elijah saw only one person standing for God; God saw 7,000 men who had not bowed to Baal. One's arithmetic will be wrong when he adds up resources from a broom tree in suicidal despair.

4. *Elijah learned that God does not become discouraged (vv. 15-16).* Don't we all feel like Elijah at times? While our spirits are low, we often make false judgments. We feel that everything has gone wrong; in our discouragement we project our feelings to the Lord and begin to believe God also has lost the battle. But He hasn't. He knows our situation. Since God's computer does not run on discouragement, Elijah, in his moment of suicidal despair learned that God is never defeated. God sees the end from the beginning and the beginning from the end; He sees beyond our moments of despair.

5. *Elijah learned that God's plans include victory (v. 17).* While Elijah saw defeat, and possibly death, God saw a place of service that would score touchdowns for His cause. Elijah's responsibility was to follow the Lord's directions, which God had already mapped out for him. God had plans for Elijah, but he could not fit into those plans while sitting in dejection. Whereas Elijah saw his own downfall, God's plans specified success. Finally, Elijah moved away from his dejected view of his life to see that suicidal defeat plus God equals victory.

A PREACHER ANGRY ENOUGH TO DIE

The Old Testament story of Jonah is about a man of God who got so angry he wanted to die (Jonah 4:1-11). God called him to go over and preach to Nineveh, a wicked city, but Jonah had other plans. So he went down to Joppa and booked passage on a ship to Tarshish, running from God. When a terrible storm was about to sink the ship, Jonah realized that his rebellion was causing the storm. When he realized that his sins were bringing trouble to innocent people, he persuaded the sailors to throw him overboard. As Jonah landed in the sea, the storm ceased and a big fish swallowed him. Inside the big fish, Jonah repented and wanted to pay his vows to the Lord.

His change of mind enabled the Lord to change Jonah's situation; the big fish headed for the shore to rid himself of his undesirable cargo. When the fish vomited Jonah up on dry land, the prophet eagerly obeyed the Lord's command, taking God's message to Nineveh. The message was one of danger—in forty days God would destroy the great city.

Happily, this message of doom changed the life of this wicked city. When the people heard God's message, four things happened throughout the city: (1) the people humbled themselves before the Lord, recognizing their dependence upon God; (2) the citizens began a program of self-denial by living sacrificial lives; (3) they turned from their evil ways by wholesale forsaking of sin; (4) they prayed for mercy by talking to the Lord about their plight; and (5) God's mercy heard the people's response and He lifted the punishment from this great city.

A sad thing then happened: Jonah became angry enough to die; the mercy of God upset him. Rather than being happy for the safety of the people, Jonah's anger was aroused because of the threat to his reputation. The response to his preaching should have pleased him but it didn't. Thus he went out on the east side of the city and sat sulking—bottling up his anger. Trouble caused Jonah to harbor his anger to a point of being suicidal.

Some people view suicide as anger turned in on one's person. Whereas murder of another person is anger inflicted on the other person, self-murder is anger inflicted on one's self. One could argue that this is what happened with Jonah; however, this is not necessarily true. Rather, Jonah was so angry that he wanted to die to get away from his life—his loss of reputation. Hundreds of people since Jonah have felt the same way he felt. Many of them have killed themselves because of their feelings of loss and humiliation.

A SOURED KING WHO KILLED HIMSELF

The people discussed in the above cases suffered the pangs of despair in their suicide crises; nevertheless, they endured the pain to survive. They overcame their crises to continue living. However, several Bible characters let their feelings of despair drive them to death (King Saul, 1 Sam. 31:4; Ahithophel, 2 Sam. 17:23; Zimri, 1 Kings 16:18; Judas, Matt. 27:5 and Acts 1:18).

King Saul is the best known example of a Bible character whose life ended in despair and suicide. When trouble overtook him, the first king of Israel lost sight of all that God had done for him. Because he saw only his troubles, he developed a warped outlook on life, changing from a nice talented hero to a pompous sourpuss. Since Saul's life is overshadowed by David, we often overlook the accomplishments of this man; he was really a dynamic leader of Israel.

Consider Saul's assets: He was the first king of Israel (1 Sam. 10:1). He had a unique body; and he was the most handsome young man in Israel (1 Sam. 9:2). He was humble and exercised self-control (1 Sam. 10:22-27). Yes, King Saul was a great man in many ways, but success ruined him; consequently, his self-will resulted in trouble.

After Saul's troubles started, his outlook changed, causing him to take his eyes off God's blessings. He then turned sour on the world; consequently, his life was downhill for his remaining days: First, there was disobedience (1 Sam. 15:4-23); next, his life became full of hatred and jealousy (1 Sam. 18:8; 19:1); he then became involved in witchcraft (1 Sam. 28:5-20). Finally, Saul committed suicide (1 Sam. 31:4). The distorted outlook of a troubled king changed his life for the worse—suicide.

Trouble caused Saul to change from a national hero to a national disgrace. What would have happened if he had grown as a person while under distress? No doubt his own life and the history of Israel would have been different. Be that as it may, Saul could not cope with his complicated life; he ended it in dishonor. Saul is an excellent example of a ruined and wasted life.

Perhaps we should ask: "What was the difference between Saul, who killed himself, and the other suicidal people in the Bible who overcame their despair?" At first this is a tough question, but closer examination reveals an important difference in Saul and the other suicidal characters. When the Lord reached down to help the other suicidal characters, they accepted help. When the Lord reached down to help Saul, he turned to witchcraft for help. Saul never learned an important principle for living his life: *One masters life as he masters himself; he masters himself as he is mastered by his Master.*

These biblical case histories give some insight into suicide. They help us see that despair does not have to mean the end of life; these people were able to overcome their despair to continue living their lives. Yet from them we learn that even a person in the service of the Lord needs special help in dealing with distress. With this insight we have a better understanding of people who struggle in despair. Thus we can now move on to an examination of suicide myths to gain even more understanding of the suicide problem.

SUICIDE MYTHS

Wouldn't it be great if someone invented a thought machine! Just attach the wires to a person's head, flip a switch, and his thoughts would flash on a monitor screen. But one's thoughts can be known only as he shares his thinking with others. Yet it isn't always with words; we know a little of what people think by what they do and say.

Our observation of people's behavior suggests that many of them hold old wives' tales about suicide; also, some people's talk reveals that they believe suicide myths. If there were a thought machine, it would flash on the monitor screen some absurd suicide beliefs.

Even though certain beliefs about suicide are debatable, many beliefs are myths; they are misconceptions; and some of them are dangerous. Edwin S. Shneidman, Ph.D., gives an excellent list of these myths which we have always heard (*Comprehensive Textbook of Psychiatry*, 1975, p. 1780). We need to be acquainted with these suicide myths, these misconceptions.

If we are to understand this complex problem of suicide, we must clear away some of these commonly held fallacies. When a person tries to help in a suicide crisis, he should understand suicide. If suicide myths cloud his thinking, the result could be disastrous, for the person who tries to help another person in such a crisis needs a clear perception of the troubled person's struggle. Counselors and pastors often hear the following five suicide myths:

■ *Myth 1: People who talk about suicide never commit the act.*

Dangling in the wind like a rag doll on a string, the body of Joe hung limply from the limb of a tree. Just the day before, he was alive; now he was dead. We stood stunned; the gruesome scene seemed so unreal. He had tied a rope around his neck, fastened the other end to the tree limb, and then jumped from a stepladder.

We had ignored Joe when he talked about killing himself; now our concern was too late. The rope had choked the life out of him. We could not bring him back to life; all we could now do was stand in horror and remember his words: "My life is empty; I have no reason for living." Only the week before this tragedy he talked about his miserable situation and said he could not bear his life.

Joe's suicide is so confusing; we did not understand what he was saying when he talked about his life. We still don't understand why he killed himself. What could we have done? I guess we are to blame, but we didn't know what to do!

The misconception that people who talk about suicide manage to stay alive is dangerous, because the opposite is true. Most people who attempt to take their own lives have talked about it.

While working at a psychiatric hospital, I interviewed hundreds of people who had attempted suicide; I cannot recall one patient who had not talked to somebody before the attempt. Over and over, as I listened to people, I realized in an increasing degree that the myth I had heard all my life is dangerous. Contrary to what I had always heard, people who attempt suicide usually talk about it before they attempt it.

While talking about his depressed wife, a man expressed this common misunderstanding. Said he, "My wife has been talking about killing herself for a month. I know that I have nothing to worry about as long as she talks about harming herself." When asked if she had said how she would kill herself, he said she talked of jumping off the bridge into the river. I asked if he cared if she jumped into the river. He replied, "Certainly I care, but she will not jump as long as she talks about jumping." I convinced the man that he was making a false assumption. The talk which he had always heard caused him to have a dangerous misconception about his wife.

I remember another husband who made the tragic mistake of believing the myth that where there is talk there will be no action. His wife had talked quite a bit about dying. He quoted her as making such remarks as, "At times I think of drowning myself. I wish that I would die. My family does not really want me with them." Even though she talked with her husband about killing herself, he did not believe that she would ever commit the act. He had always heard that people who talk about harming themselves never do it. It shocked him when she put a gun to her head and pulled the trigger to end her life.

■ *Myth 2: Suicide happens without any warning.* The belief that suicide happens without warning is not true, as most people who kill themselves have warned of their intentions. In fact, suicidal people usually give many clues and warnings, several of which will be discussed. Regretfully, much too often nobody hears or notices these warning signals, or the warnings are taken lightly or ignored. Members of a suicide victim's family hear when it is too late. Pastors and Sunday School teachers frequently hear warnings of suicidal intentions and ignore them. Later they live with guilty feelings because they did not take the warning signals seriously.

Mrs. Adams was an excellent Sunday School teacher. She spent many hours studying in preparation for teaching her class, and kept in contact with class members. People knew her as a teacher who really cared about people. When any of the ladies had a problem, they felt comfortable in talking with her about it. This teacher not only did an exceptional work as a Sunday School teacher, but also lived her Christian life day by day.

One day something happened to make this fine teacher miserable. A member of the class casually said: "I sometimes feel that I am in the way; it is as though my family doesn't really need me. There have been times when I wanted to end it all." Mrs. Adams responded: "You are, of course, just kidding. Snap out of it; stop feeling sorry for yourself."

She thought no more of the conversation until she heard the sad news that her friend had died from an overdose of pills. It was then that she realized that she had failed to really listen to her friend's warning. In fact, Mrs. Adams felt that she had "slammed an emotional door in the woman's face." She had taken lightly the woman's cry for help.

■ *Myth 3: A suicidal person wants to be dead.* We have all played it or have seen it on TV. Tug-of-war requires that those on each side of a line, with a large rope stretching between them, try to pull the other team across the line. The successful team rejoices as their opponents finally lose ground and fall in defeat.

This tug-of-war also goes on in the minds of suicidal people. There is the continuous tug between life and escape from life. The person wants to live, but does not want to assume responsibility for living. The side that pulls the other side over wins. If the side that wants escape wins, it means attempted suicide. If the side that wants life wins, it means survival.

The belief that a suicidal person wants to be dead is a myth. I have heard it said, "He wants to kill himself; you cannot do anything to stop him." Granted, suicide is a tough subject. Who can understand the feelings of a person in a suicide crisis? But you can be sure, a person who attempts suicide does not want to be *dead!* For the person in a suicide struggle, it is not a matter of wanting to *die*, but actually *a desire to get away from life.*

When we view suicide as escape from life rather than desire for death, we expose this commonly held myth. Really, the person who attempts suicide, seems to have ambivalent feelings—two opposite feelings at the same time. On the one hand, he wants to get away from life by dying. It is a frantic effort to escape a life that is so painful, he feels he cannot bear it any longer. Death he sees as escape from the hurt and pain of existence. On the other hand, he has an opposite strong feeling, a desire to live. Thus he wants to die to escape a painful life, but at the same time wants somebody to save him from death.

Consequently, the thinking of a person in a suicide crisis is strange. He makes plans to destroy himself, and at the same time has fantasies that someone will rescue him. Most of the people who commit suicide die believing, hoping that somebody at the last minute will come to their rescue. Again, the person in the suicide crisis does not want to die; he wants to escape the pain of life.

A tragedy at a hospital where I worked illustrates how a person can experience opposite feelings simultaneously. A teenage girl had a desire to escape life; she also had a desire for somebody to save her from death. The tragedy happened while a nurse was giving medicine to the patients. During the time the patients were in line to receive medication, this teenage girl rushed past the patients and the nurse, picked up a handful of pills and swallowed them. She wanted to escape life but also felt someone would save her from death; she thought that hospital personnel would pump her stomach to remove the pills. How could anyone possibly die of an overdose in a hospital? True, they pumped her stomach, but she died of complications.

This precious little girl died and did not really want to be dead. The saying that a suicidal person wants to die, and nothing can be done to stop him, is a myth. This girl wanted to escape the intense emotional pain of existence, while at the same time she wanted someone to rescue her. Nevertheless, this feeling does not keep one alive. If rescue fails, one is just as dead, regardless of the dream that someone will come to the rescue.

■ *Myth 4: A suicidal person is suicidal for life.* The belief that once a person is suicidal he is suicidal for the rest of his life needs correcting. True, one may be predisposed to suicide for a lifetime, but the acute crisis, or period of extreme danger is usually a short time. It is a period of hours or days, not months or years. It is important to keep in mind that a person may live for years with a chronic suicide struggle, but he will not live even a few months in a suicide crisis.

Just suppose that a friend calls to tell you that he has a loaded pistol to his head. One of three things will happen to the friend: he will get help to protect him from himself; he will cool off and gain control of himself; or, he will kill himself. The bottom line in the acute crisis is definite;

someone will rescue the person; personality factors will enable him to handle the crisis; or he will pull the trigger of the pistol and injure or kill himself. He will not remain in the acute crisis indefinitely.

There are at least three possibilities for a person in a suicide crisis. (1) One may come out of a crisis and three months later kill himself; (2) he may come out of the acute crisis and live for years predisposed to suicide, or he may survive because of other personality factors that counteract his need to escape life; (3) he may come out of the acute crisis to live predisposed to suicide, but never again have stress factors to trigger an acute suicide crisis.

■ *Myth 5: All suicidal people are mentally ill.* I once arranged for a graduate student to come to a hospital where I worked to talk with some schizophrenic patients. When the young man arrived, I was not immediately available, and he had to wait for some time for me. While waiting, he talked with a schizophrenic patient who was doing some office work. As the patient was neatly dressed and well educated, the graduate student did not realize that he was a patient; so he asked him: "Do you have many schizophrenics here at the hospital?" The patient replied: "No, I have not seen any." The student was surprised when he found out later that he was talking with a schizophrenic.

Similarly, some people expect that a mentally ill person will be someone totally out of control and that a suicidal person will be deranged.

Consider several facts before we discuss the myth that all suicidal people are mentally ill. One, a person may be mentally ill without being suicidal. Two, a person may be suicidal without being mentally ill—psychotic. Three, an outward show of disturbance is often not present in a person who kills himself. Four, there are certain types of mental illness when the sick person needs protection from himself.

The myth that all suicidal people are mentally ill poses this familiar question: "Is a person mentally ill who kills himself?" The definition of the word mentally ill is important in answering this question. Perhaps a better question would be, Is a person who kills himself psychotic? That is, is his behavior characterized by defective or lost contact with reality?

Even this question lends itself to more than one interpretation; for mental illness is not the opposite of mental health, and people interpret mental illness differently. This is to say two things: a person who is not mentally ill may not be mentally healthy; and some people consider mental illness and emotional disturbance as one and the same. That one can be emotionally disturbed without being psychotic does not change the definition for some people. *Be that as it may, many people who attempt suicide are not psychotic.* That is, their behavior is not characterized by defective or lost contact with reality.

To say that a person attempting suicide is mentally competent could be a different matter. Would anyone consider a person mentally competent when suicidal thoughts enter and take over his thinking? Would anyone consider a person mentally competent when he kills himself to escape life? He chooses nonexistence rather than his painful existence on earth.

As one can see, the question of sanity in suicide has no easy answers. Nevertheless, clinical data document three facts: (1) There will not always be visible emotional or mental disturbance in a person who kills himself; (2) it is a myth that all people who kill themselves are mentally ill, if one means psychotic; (3) some mentally ill people do kill themselves.

Correction of myths does help in understanding suicide; yet there is still so much misunderstanding about this human tragedy. Better understanding would help heal the hurt of people who have this problem. Perhaps the examination of suicide beliefs in the next chapter will give more insight into the suicide controversy.

MOST PEOPLE UNDERSTAND ENOUGH TO GET HELP

When one has learned everything he can learn about suicide, there is still much he does not know; still, one can understand enough to get help. Lack of knowledge should not keep us from trying to get assistance for people who need it. John Eckenroth, a fine Christian public school principal, feeling helpless when his school faced a suicide crisis, prevented a more serious tragedy; he called on someone who knew what to do.

In only a few days, life in Harlem, a small town 100 miles

southeast of Atlanta, experienced a drastic change after a student committed suicide. Night after night many parents had frightening nightmares as they observed the fear, hurt, and confusion of their own teenagers. Administrators and teachers at the Harlem Middle School lived in constant fear of what could happen. A sense of tension filled the air, along with the main topic of conversation—suicide. Would Harlem Middle School experience a cluster of senseless self-murders? The principal tells how the crisis developed:

He had been at our school only three weeks. We knew so little about him; yet what we did know was very good. He appeared to be a fine young man, an "A" student. He would likely have been on one of our athletic teams in the fall. Nevertheless, such is not to be, because this "A" student now lies in silent death.

Then Mr. Eckenroth went on to tell how he and his staff dealt with students in the wake of the tragedy:

In the beginning we thought we had a very small problem involving only three students. However, our thinking changed as we worked through our health classes to identify students having a problem with suicide. Quickly the three changed to eight or ten suicidal students. Then, in just a few days the number of students experiencing trouble with suicide increased to twenty-five. Their involvement ranged from troublesome thoughts about harming themselves to attempted suicide.

When we became involved with our students after the tragedy, we discovered that three students had taken an overdose of pills at home. A couple of students cut their wrists. But most of the students involved struggled with thoughts of harming themselves. Many students came to teachers, saying: "I just don't want to live"; also, several parents found suicide notes. The volume of this problem indicates that it was not a mild one; we had a serious situation. The two cases below are typical ones.

One student came to the office and asked to see me; he was very upset. He said, "I am having thoughts of harming myself, and I know of several other students who are having these terrible thoughts." This boy had been at our school for two years; he had never given any trouble or indicated that he was disturbed; he had been one of our best students.

A teenage girl came to my office. She was frightened and was crying. She suddenly blurted out: "I finally admitted something to myself; I admitted that my father killed himself when I was a little girl. Since his death I have felt so ashamed, but nobody ever spent any time with me. I have not talked about my feelings; now I am having thoughts of doing what Daddy did." I went four times to her home to make certain that she got help.

Harlem Middle School Principal Eckenroth averted further suicides in his school because he was willing to admit that he needed professional help. First, he called in a trained person to talk to the students in a voluntary assembly. Out of 540 students (grades six through eight) eligible to attend the assembly, over 500 attended. Even though some of the students probably attended to get out of class, many of them went because of real concerns. After the twenty-minute assembly, thirty-five students stayed to ask questions. They asked such questions as: "Was it wrong not to cry at his funeral?"/"What is the least painful way to kill one's self?"/"Will I go to jail for trying to commit suicide?"

After the initial confrontation of the crisis, the principal took other positive steps: he involved parents to give support to his school during its time of stress. He worked with parents and mental health resources to get referrals for students needing help. He used mental health professionals for workshops to inform and guide teachers and others in dealing with the crisis.

This middle school principal said: "I did not know what to do when we had the outbreak of suicide attempts, but I found someone who helped us prevent a cluster of suicides." He was alert, and alerted others to a very tense community problem. His alertness likely saved several teenagers from committing suicide.

This principal believes that other schools throughout the country may be emotional powder kegs, waiting to be ignited. He does not consider that his school is much different from hundreds of other schools; therefore, he readily agrees that the United States is in a suicide epidemic. He believes that the crisis at Harlem could happen in many other American schools. Likewise, he believes that other principals can get help to prevent suicide; he believes there is hope for the hopeless.

Teenage suicide in Plano, Texas, beginning in February 1983, moved teenagers and adults to give emergency help for distraught young people. This community experienced eight teenage suicides in sixteen months. These teens even tended to copy the suicide methods of other teens who had killed themselves: Four of them used carbon-monoxide poisoning to end their lives; three killed themselves with guns. Students were so concerned about the outbreak of suicide that they set up two support groups—BIONIC and SWAT. BIONIC stands for Believe It Or Not I Care; SWAT stands for Students Working All Together. Adults were so alarmed they conceived and implemented a twenty-four-hour emergency line to help troubled teenagers. The people in Plano knew enough to get help for their teenagers.

CONCLUSION

Is ignorance bliss? It certainly is not bliss in the suicide epidemic; rather, often results in tragedy. Lack of information and understanding cause people to say and do the wrong things. On the other hand, informed people are able to make a positive approach to this problem; they can offer hope to hopeless people. Be that as it may, almost any person knows enough to find somebody who does know what to do; in situations when a person does not know what to do, he ought to admit his lack of knowledge and ask for help. Rumblings of concern are being heard in some school systems in which the people are saying: "We don't know what to do, but we want to know. Where can we find help? Where can we get reliable information?"

The next chapter discusses various beliefs about suicide and ways people interpret self-murder.

3 HOW PEOPLE INTERPRET SUICIDE

A grandmother, watching her grandson in a parade, saw him as a perfect boy. A hundred boys dressed in bright uniforms marched up one street and down another. Ninety-nine boys marched together, but one boy, Jack, her grandson, was out of step with the other boys. When they put down a left foot, he put down a right foot. Hundreds whispered to each other, "Look, one boy is out of step."

Jack's family, including the extended family, eagerly watched as the boys approached where they were standing. When the hundred boys approached the family, his grandmother cried: "Look, look! All the boys are out of step but Jack!"

This story illustrates how people interpret information in different ways. We sometimes see what we want to see and hear what we want to hear. Our thinking influences our interpretation of any situation; therefore, we interpret suicide according to our background, needs, and philosophy of life. Consequently, our world is full of different beliefs about suicide.

Nonetheless, recently there is more sympathy for troubled people, including suicidal people. Perhaps much of this change in attitude is due to mass media publicity of the suicide epidemic, especially the coverage given suicides among teenagers and farmers. Even so, much still needs to be done in the area of suicide. Many people still view a suicidal person as a nut, seeking attention. Such a view is usually wrong; this stereotype is in no way characteristic of most suicidal people.

How do people interpret the personal consequences of suicide? The attitudes toward this tragedy are perhaps the most controversial and complicated of all the aspects of existence. They range all the way from a view of suicide as the highest achievement and glory a person can attain, to the view of suicide as a deadly sin for which there is no forgiveness. I can think of few subjects with so many different opinions. Let's consider a few of these views.

SELF-MURDER CONDONED

The belief that there are times and circumstances when it is right to end one's life is stronger than many people realize. Nevertheless, this view is not new to history (see *The New Shaff-Herzog Encyclopedia of Religious Knowledge*, XI, 1911, p. 132). Greek Stoicism placed little value on life and advocated death as a means of "freeing the soul." People in the early Roman Empire also defended the view that suicide is right; the Roman stoic Seneca expressed this view. In Japanese society self-murder is generally considered to be an honorable act; in World War II many Japanese pilots committed suicide by crashing planes into American ships.

More recently there has been a renewed interest in one's right to kill himself. There is a movement among some physicians, philosophers, lawyers, and even theologians, to legalize voluntary euthanasia. This law would permit a physician to help a person experience voluntary death.

One advocate of voluntary death, Doris Portwood, says: "I might commit suicide if I went blind or had to be dependent on other people. If in great pain with cancer, I would commit suicide. But I would never turn to suicide out of simple depression" (*Augusta Herald*, April 23, 1986).

The recent suicide missions in Lebanon gave a drastic demonstration of self-inflicted death for a purpose. These suicide missions killed many American men. Even though these missions were foolish and cruel, they demonstrate belief in one's right to take his life.

It is possible that some may interpret the suicide missions in Lebanon as similar to the martyrs of the early church. By so doing, one will make a false interpretation, since early Christians were murdered at the hand of others because of their commitment to their Lord. A person who drives a truck loaded with dynamite into an American Embassy dies because of commitment to his country.

These references reveal there are people who believe it right to take one's life under certain conditions. Even though their reasons differ, all of them believe that it is permissible to kill one's self.

SELF-MURDER CONDEMNED

In 1790 John Wesley was very concerned about suicide in England. He believed there was no country in the habitable world with as high a rate of suicide as England. However, few people would now accept his solution to the problem; most people would reject it as cruel and unjust. At any rate, this great Christian suggested an outrageous method for discouraging self-murder:

> But how can this vile abuse of the law be prevented, and this execrable crime effectually discouraged? By a very easy method. We read in ancient history that, at a certain period, many of the women of Sparta murdered themselves. This fury increasing, a law was made that the body of every woman who killed herself should be exposed naked in the streets. The fury ceased at once.
>
> Only let a law be made and rigorously executed, that the body of every self-murderer, Lord or peasant, shall be hanged in chains, and the English fury will cease at once (*The Works of John Wesley*, Baker Book House, 1979, vol. 13, p. 481).

The general view that life is sacred and that self-murder is wrong also includes points of difference. The early Greeks came under this general rule as they considered suicide as unnatural and criminal; Plato and Aristotle gave great emphasis to this view (Harold Kaplan and Benjamin Sadock, *Comprehensive Textbook of Psychiatry* II, Williams and Wilkins, 1975, p. 1,774).

What does the Bible say about self-murder? Neither the Old Testament nor the New Testament gives specific prohibition against suicide; yet certain passages such as Romans 14:7-9, 1 Corinthians 6:19, and Ephesians 5:29 might be considered in connection with self-murder. Saint Augustine (A.D. 354-430) believed that the Bible taught it was wrong to kill one's self. He strongly rejected suicide, because it removed hope of repentance and violated the commandment that prohibited killing (*Ibid*).

The action at the Council of Toledo (A.D. 693) depicted the sentiment of the Church at that time; the action also reflected the attitude of the church for many years to come. The Council action stipulated that a person who attempted to kill himself would be excommunicated (*Ibid.*). Church action often resulted in persecution for those who attempted suicide; and it often resulted in sorrow for the survivors of suicide victims. Nevertheless, the view of suicide as sin has influenced the thinking of society for hundreds of years.

SELF-MURDER INTERPRETED

God created every person different from every other person; consequently, people interpret life and death differently. This fact is well illustrated by the conversation of two women. One woman said: "I am glad that every person is different." "Why?" asked the second woman. "Because," said the first woman, "if everybody was like me, everyone would want my husband." "I know," said the second woman, "but if everybody was like me, nobody would want your husband."

Advice about salvation and suicide has taken on new meaning since Kenneth Nally killed himself after being counseled by pastors of Grace Community Church, Panorama City, California. Nally's parents sued because counselors told him that if he was saved he would go to heaven even if he killed himself. Notwithstanding that a judge dismissed this malpractice suit against clergy, the legal suit emphasizes that one's interpretation of salvation and suicide is important (*Christian Century*, May 29, 1985).

Early in my life, I faced this complicated aspect of suicide in an unusual way. When I returned one morning from speaking on a local radio station, my wife met me at the door with an emergency. She had just had a phone call from a man who was crying; he told her that he was about to kill himself. When he heard me speaking on the radio a few minutes earlier, he grabbed at the last straw. He pleaded with my wife on the phone: "Please get your husband to help me. I don't want to live, but I don't want to die."

I drove across town to his home, and he was waiting for me at the door. As soon as we were seated in his home, he began to unravel his tragic story. "Five months ago my wife and I sat in this very room," he said. "I sat where I am now sitting; she sat where you are sitting. We had come to the end of another day and it was time for our evening devotion." The man rose from his chair, went across the room to a desk, and returned with an open Bible. He then continued, "This is the Bible she used for our devotion; I have kept it open since that fatal night."

The Bible was open at the eighth chapter of Romans. Handing me the Bible, he asked me to read the chapter. I read the passage, ending with the great promise that nothing will separate us from the love of God. He then dropped a theological bombshell, asking one of the hardest questions I had ever faced.

"After my wife finished reading that same Scripture, we retired for the night. At 2 o'clock in the morning, the sheriff woke me to tell me they had found my wife in her automobile, out in the country, dead. Obviously, she did not go to bed, but drove her automobile to that lonely spot and killed herself." Then he asked, "Where is my wife, in heaven or in hell?" You talk about squirming; I was really in the hot seat.

At that time, I could not rely on years of training in human behavior and experience with suicidal people. Even with all theological and philosophical speculation put aside, this was a no-win question. I knew enough to understand that if I said she went to hell, he would sink deeper into despair, and probably end his life. If I told him that she went to heaven, he would want to kill himself to join her. Instead of giving him a clear answer, I focused on a solution to his own tangled life.

While many people subscribe to the view that life is valuable and sacred, they often ask, "If a Christian kills himself, is he saved or lost?" What is the answer? Let's seek a solution as we examine beliefs related to suicide.

■ *Self-murder is unforgiveable.* Most people who believe this base their position on the second commandment, which forbids murder, and the impossibility of forgiveness after death.

I have seen suicidal people for therapy who used this belief to stay alive. They stated, "I would kill myself, but I know that I would land in hell." Perhaps one should be careful of expressing an opposite view to a person in a suicide crisis. If he is restrained from self-harm by this fear, one could remove the last resistance and cause the person to kill himself.

On the contrary, one may be so dogmatic in expressing the beliefs there is no hope for the suicide victim that he cause innocent survivors to suffer needless hurt. First-hand experience with such a case made me excessively sensitive to the possibility of inflicting such pain.

A man I'll call Thomas asked for help because he was "beginning to believe there is no God." Even though his wife was an active member of a church, he professed no religion. Thomas' trouble began when he was eight years of age, when his father killed himself. His father had been sick since a "nervous breakdown" on the battlefield during a war; he was waiting to be admitted to a psychiatric hospital at the time of the tragedy.

Though Thomas' father was mentally ill, the neighbors were dogmatic in their opinions about his eternal destination. While sitting up with his corpse, they expressed these dogmatic opinions. And, as often happens, they did not see the little eight-year-old boy who listened to their conversation. Some said, "It is terrible that a good man, who lived all this time for the Lord, has now gone to hell because he killed himself." This struck daggers in the boy's heart. The neighbors never knew the agony of the little boy who ran off into the dark to cry.

Though Thomas had had other traumatic relationships, this frightening experience when his father was a corpse, gave rootage to the doubt that now disturbed him. When Thomas' immoral behavior left him with strong guilt, this experience became a full-blown problem. The guilt and early experience weighed heavily on him. How could he relate to a God who had sent his father to hell after he had served Him for years? How could he get forgiveness without relating to God?

Consequently, the anxiety and threat to Thomas' ego activated his denial mechanism. If his mental mechanism could get rid of the existence of God, the threat of punishment would be lessened. So when Thomas came for help, he was dominated by three strong feelings: hostility toward

God, fear of punishment for his sin, and doubt of God's existence. The dogmatic expression of the belief that all people who kill themselves are forever lost, left permanent emotional scars in the life of a bereaved eight-year-old boy.

■ *A person who kills himself is crazy.* One theological position is: "No person in his right mind would kill himself." Based on this belief, people reason that one who kills himself is not responsible or accountable for his behavior. The reasoning continues: "God would consider an incompetent person innocent; so, if a person is a Christian and kills himself, he will go to heaven." One who holds this belief must deal with this complicated question: Was the suicide victim emotionally, mentally, and spiritually incompetent? There are not, of course, any easy answers to this question, for nobody can really know the emotional, mental, and spiritual condition of a person who kills himself.

Research, however, has indicated that many people who attempt suicide are not mentally ill, in the sense of being psychotic; that is, their behavior is not characterized by defective or lost contact with reality. Furthermore, the data suggests that many people kill themselves with no outward show of emotional disturbance. But, who can know the emotional, mental, and spiritual condition of the person at the moment he takes his life? One thing is certain: the person who brings his earthly life to an end is overcome by the pain of his separate existence. There is no easy, satisfying solution to this question.

■ *A truly saved person will not kill himself.* This position, closely related to the above belief, affirms that a born-again person will overcome a suicide crisis. Some people with this interpretation do not accept even mental illness as an exception. Rather, many people state that mental illness is caused by personal sin. Consequently, if a person kills himself as a result of mental illness, personal sin caused his mental illness and eventually his suicide. Please remember though, people who believe that a Christian will not kill himself do not necessarily believe that personal sin causes mental illness.

Further, if one believes that personal sin causes mental illness, does he also believe that personal sin causes physical illness? "But," someone may respond, "so much mental illness is caused by mental or emotional conflict." Granted, but so is much physical illness caused by mental or emotional conflict. When one accepts that mental illness is punishment for personal sin, he should accept that physical illness is punishment for personal sin.

As to the matter of a Christian taking his life, everyone is on his own to settle the matter for himself. Because of the sacredness of life and spiritual resources, a Christian should be able to cope with life. Yet, is it possible for even a Christian to suffer such emotional pain because of his separate existence that he sees no way out other than death? An answer to this controversial question is perhaps beyond the scope and range of human speculation.

■ *Suicide causes a saved person to lose his salvation.* One theological position on suicide is the belief that once a person has become a true Christian, there is nothing, not even self-inflicted death, that can separate him from God's love to cause him to be lost. This position considers personal salvation, from beginning to end, as based on the grace of God, rather than on the works of the person. People with this belief base their belief on such Bible passages as Romans 8:31-39 and John 10:27-30.

There are two strong positions against this position. One opposite position consists of those who believe in the doctrine of eternal security but who maintain that "a person who kills himself did not get saved." The other opposite position affirms that a saved person can lose his salvation and finally be lost. Therefore, according to the latter belief, even a true Christian can kill himself and thereby lose his salvation.

People in both of these positions refer to Scriptures which condemn murder. They point out that an unrepentant murderer is not a Christian; and a person who kills himself has no opportunity for repentance for self-murder; therefore, the dead person cannot repent of suicide to become a Christian. The position that not even suicide will cause a Christian to lose his salvation has its theological problems and opponents. This position, as well as the previous ones, is very controversial and complicated.

A CHRISTIAN APPROACH TO SUICIDE

Three small children sat before a television watching a complicated soap opera. As the show was dealing with a story of two men who had been married to the same woman, the family conflicts were far beyond the children's understanding. Yet the show was especially interesting to the children because of a conversation they had heard that very day. Their mothers had been discussing the mothers' relationship to each other. They had explained to the children that they were sisters-in-law, because they had married brothers. As their husband's mother was present, they had also explained how the mothers were kin to the children's grandmother; they told the children that their grandmother was their mother-in-law.

Excited by the in-law stories which they had heard, they were soaking up the television soap opera. Finally one little boy asked: "What kin are they?" One of the others replied: "They are no kin; they were just married to the same wife." "Oh, yes, they are kin," replied the third little boy; "they are husbands-in-law."

As we try to determine our relationship to the suicide epidemic, our relationship, like the soap opera, is very complicated. Christians have been trying to interpret the personal consequences of suicide since the beginning of the Christian church. Yet one can see from this chapter that throughout Christian history people have arrived at different interpretations. Christians now living, and facing a suicide epidemic, do not have the luxury of sitting on the sidelines of life to second-guess God; we must meet the challenge of this suicide epidemic. Christians can meet this challenge with the following suggestions:

■ *We are not the judge of suicide victims*. Whatever the personal consequences of suicide, the God of love and justice will judge human behavior. The Christian task is to meet the challenge of the suicide epidemic and leave judgment with the Lord. When I am tempted to judge people who have committed suicide, a verse from the Bible helps control my thinking: "Who shall lay any thing to the charge of God's elect? It is God that justifieth" (Rom. 8:33).

No person, regardless of training, is qualified to judge the life and death of another human being. Unless one has walked in the shoes and struggled with the problems of another person, he does not know the person's situation. And, of course, no person has lived the life of a person who struggles with suicide; every person lives his own life. I, for one, am glad to leave the judging with the Lord.

■ *We cannot escape the Christian challenge of the suicide epidemic.* Whatever the personal consequences of suicide, the Christian task is to interpret and use Christian resources for meeting the basic need of suicidal people. Perhaps one reason for so many different views about suicide is the focus of our society, especially the focus of theology. We deal with the symptoms and tragedy of suicide, rather than with the underlying problem.

The basic problem of the suicidal person is his fear of life; he is unable to cope with his separate existence; he cannot assume responsibility for living. Certainly the symptoms and suffering of self-murder are real and need our attention. Nevertheless, progress in finding a solution to suicide will require focus on the underlying cause, along with the symptoms and suffering. That is, we will make significant progress in dealing with suicide, when we deal with the basic struggle of human existence.

This basic struggle is with the inner storm of one's soul. Life falls apart on the inside before it does on the outside. The fundamental issue in dealing with suicide is the agonizing emotional pain of the person who tries to take his life. This pain is caused by the person's inability to cope with life.

Even though the deadly act of suicide wraps itself in much mystery, we can understand it. As we move into the next chapter, some of this mystery will be unraveled. We will ask, and try to answer this question: Why does a person kill himself? Perhaps by so doing we shall gain a better understanding of suicide to learn our relationship to the suicide epidemic.

4 WHY DO PEOPLE KILL THEMSELVES?

Imagine a teenage girl traveling a rough, winding road suddenly coming upon a big sign, "STOP! BRIDGE WASHED OUT." Nearby, another sign reads, "DETOUR," and an arrow points to another road to take. The young traveler must now make a crucial decision, one that should be evident. However, if she ignores the signs, doubtlessly she will lose her life in the dark, murky river. But by observing the signs, she could continue her travel by another route and eventually get back on the main highway.

A person in a suicide crisis is somewhat like the teenager. While traveling the rough winding road of life, a suicidal person eventually arrives at a washed-out bridge—suicide crisis. If he continues straight ahead, he becomes a suicide casualty in the dark, murky waters of death. If he finds, or somebody helps him find, the detour out of the crisis, he will eventually get back on the main road of life.

In this chapter we will determine the factors and forces which wash out the bridge on life's rough, winding road. We will examine the causes of self-murder to gain insight into the suicide epidemic. Our task is not easy, but it is essential to our understanding of this human tragedy.

Because of the suicide epidemic, many are asking this penetrating question, "Why does a person kill himself?" Over and over a father and mother whose son or daughter committed the fatal act ask this question. Often a child whose parent committed suicide asks this painful question. When one of their number ends his life, church members ask, "Why did he do it?" Frequently co-workers ask this question when a fellow worker kills himself. This question is familiar to all of us.

Certain information about a suicidal person will give, at least, a partial answer. This answer does not lump all suicidal people into one mold, for those who attempt to kill themselves are individually different. And each person experiences different kinds and degrees of stress. Yet there is unique information on people who attempt suicide. This special information will help to answer the question, "Why did he/she commit suicide?"

For those who care and want to help people in suicide crises, it is imperative that we understand the cause of this problem. What brings a person to a point in life that death seems better than life? To answer this question, we need to have at least some knowledge of the origin and development of the suicide crisis. An examination of the root of the suicide crisis, the feelings of a person in a suicide crisis, and the factors which cause a suicide crisis will help us understand people who come to this state of despair. And, this information will give us a new appreciation of a suicidal person's struggle.

SUICIDE IS AN EFFORT TO ESCAPE LIFE

Many people are fascinated by a little bird, the woodpecker. This particular bird often gets our attention by disturbing the quietness of a forest with the sound of its pecking on dead trees. No other bird, being so small, makes such a loud noise. So if a bird can be proud of its achievement, the woodpecker would probably be a very conceited bird.

One day, as the story goes, a woodpecker was pecking away on a big tree, when suddenly a bolt of lightning struck the tree and split it from the top to the bottom. The woodpecker died thinking that he had done all the damage to the tree!

Sometimes we, like the woodpecker, get carried away with the importance of what we are doing. As far as we are concerned the world revolves around our pet projects; the world turns on our interests and desires. Little do we realize that we are small woodpeckers, pecking away at the issues of life. Often we are not aware of the lightning striking around us. We do not see all the factors and forces which influence our lives.

Life is so big and complicated. When we consider all that is known, it is only a small part of the total body of knowledge. Dealing with the issues of life and death, we recognize that we know so little. Even if we knew everything that is known by humans, we would have only touched the tip of the real meaning of life.

Therefore, as we come to a discussion of the why of suicide, we need to tread softly lest our feelings of self-sufficiency keep us from seeing many unseen forces which affect our lives. If one is to feel humble, let him feel humble in dealing with life's struggles. When we hear of a suicide tragedy, we should say: "It is by the grace of God that I am not a suicide victim." Indeed, it is only by the grace of God that life does not overcome all of us. With such a humble attitude, we come now to ask and answer the following question: Why does a person kill himself?

The reasons appear simple, but they are very complex. They are complex, because they all flow into one specific reason: one kills himself to bring to an end his miserable existence; by the suicide act the person seeks to end his life. One person who had attempted suicide said, "I wanted to kiss this old world good-bye."

Thus the suicide crisis is rooted in humanity's inherited endowment. Persons want to escape a life that seems unbearable; they want to renounce membership in the human race. Yet no human act, not even suicide, can free one from one's inherited humanity. Still, hundreds of people every year continue their efforts to escape by killing themselves. Discussion of two inescapable conditions inherited by every person—human frailty and human aloneness, may help clarify the why of suicide.

HUMAN FRAILTY

■ *There is no escape from humanity.* First, let us examine human frailty as the origin of the suicide crisis. Please permit a personal challenge: Step off a few paces from yourself and take a look at your humanity. You must never forget that you are made from the dust of the earth; neither must you forget that God breathed into you the breath of life and you became a living soul. You must never forget that you are created in the image of God. You must never forget that you are a creature of time; neither must you forget that you are a creature of eternity.

You exist between dust and Deity, between time and eternity. If you move out of balance in either direction, trouble results. If you center your life on either one, to the exclusion of the other, life loses its equilibrium. Should you sink to the level of animal living, your life would fail its intended purpose. Should you try to play God, your life and the lives of others would be in jeopardy. You are pulled between dust and Deity, between animal and God, between time and eternity; you are a human being.

One must pay the price of one's humanity. He is subject to the needs, hurts, desires, and hopes of the human race. The common frailties of humanity are his. He is in the middle of life's tragedies and triumphs. The raw material of human existence is his life involvement. Because one is human, he is subject to hostility, fear, doubt, insecurity, jealousy, envy, guilt, and misery. Because one is human, he is capable of courage, gaiety, love, peace, hope, and happiness. His need for love, achievement, and purpose is real.

A human learns the meaning, the value, and the truth of life as he filters it through his own individual experience. A human has goals for his life, feels the hurt of human experience, and knows the joys of human ecstasy and the thrills of human adventure. The human life consists of work and play, joy and sorrow, peace and war, laughing and crying, sickness and health, hurt and healing, meditation and madness, worship and rebellion. He can walk the higher or lower road of human existence. In such is rooted suicide.

■ *There is no cover-up with God.* Though a human has difficulty accepting the attributes and limitations of humanity, the Bible sets forth unsparingly the weak as well as the strong among God's children. No effort is made in Holy Writ to deny, evade, or cover up human frailties. It reveals humans with the veneer peeled off. It tells of their climb to the top and their fall to the bottom.

The Old Testament gives the assets and liabilities of humans. Abraham, depicted as the chosen of God and the leader of men, is also depicted as a man who lied to save his own skin (Gen. 12:11-13). He also cooperated in his wife's work to take over the work of God by permitting him to have a child by another woman (Gen. 16:3). Look at Jacob (Gen. 25:29–50:14). No other Bible character represents more fully than he the conflicts within human nature; yet the history of this man's career leaves no doubt that he was a chosen instrument of God in spite of his conflicts. Gideon, who stood up to the mighty foes of Israel in war, could not handle prosperity in time of peace (Jud. 8:24-31). The moral range of human nature is illustrated graphically by the rise and fall of David (1 Sam. 17:25-53; Ps. 51). The Bible paints a picture of progress under the Solomon of wisdom (1 Kings 4:29-30), but a picture of failure under the Solomon who exercised no self-control (1 Kings 11:1-13).

The adventures of the prophets reveal the attributes and limitations of God's children. Among pictorial scenes of great adventure, Elijah, who had fled from a woman, is pictured under a juniper tree in the wilderness, sitting in discouragement and exhaustion, wanting to give up and die (1 Kings 19:1-8). Jonah, a strong mixture of strength and weakness, was so concerned about damage to his reputation that he wanted to die (Jonah 4:1-3). Jeremiah, so passionate that he was called the weeping prophet, came to a time in life when he cursed the day of his birth, wished he had died in the womb, and seemingly longed to return to the womb (Jer. 20:14-18). Suicide is rooted in human frailty.

Although the world of these men was far different from ours, none would deny that the struggle of human nature is the same. The needs for self-preservation and self-propagation in Abraham are still basic human needs. Neither did the conflicts of human nature cease with the death of Jacob. Brave Gideons continue to stand erect under the fire of opposition and fall under the impact of blessings. Modern Davids meet difficult problems because of the same failure of self-control. Thrilling adventures leave some modern Elijahs with a frightening aloneness. Reputation continues to be more important than life for some modern Jonahs. The pressure of strong opposition can still push an outgoing Jeremiah into repressed infantile behavior.

■ *There is no enslavement in a blind fate.* Every person has the potential for meeting and mastering life; human frailty does not have to be human fatality. True, in every generation people suffer the pangs and delights of being human. Yet, notwithstanding the sorrows, tragedies, uncertainties, and inequalities of human living, life has much to offer for those who are brave enough to meet its challenge.

Sad, sad, many are not able to meet its challenge; some yearn for a way to escape it; millions try to escape it by suicide.

Their need to escape is rooted in the struggle of human frailty. When the tension and stress of life overcome them, they sink in the sea of despair. Unable to cope with the inner and outer storm, they end up in a suicide crisis. The suicide victim is not seeking death; he is seeking escape from human frailty.

I once heard a speaker tell of two babies, born about the same time, with disfigured, ugly faces. In time, as they grew up, they looked at themselves in the mirror and realized that they were much different from other people. One was overcome by his appearance, and finally went out and hanged himself. The other person, knowing that his appearance was homely, went out and made a million dollars on his unsightly face.

I know not whether this story was true, or if it was used only to illustrate a point in the speaker's lecture. Regardless, it does illustrate a point in our present discussion. Many people transform human frailty into forces for triumphant living; others let human frailties transform them into victims of despair.

ALONENESS—THE SOLITARY SELF

A little boy once expressed his alarming and painful feeling of aloneness—the terror of a solitary self. His mother heard him crying in the middle of the night. She went to his room and asked: "Joe, what is wrong?" He replied: "I am afraid." His mother consoled him: "Darling, nothing will bother you; don't be afraid." "I know," said Joe, "I am not afraid of nothing. I am afraid when I think of just me."

■ *Human aloneness frightens us.* Little Joe speaks for all of us. For we too are afraid when we think of our aloneness. We know that we exist apart from our world and this knowledge makes us afraid. We know that we exist apart from every other person and this also frightens us. Because we are apart from everything and everybody, we feel lonely and afraid. In the case of our separate existence, what we know does hurt us. Loneliness is not a disease; it is an alarming and frightening feeling.

■ *Human aloneness is inherited by all of us.* Aloneness

is the interest of philosophers, therapists, theologians, and the experience of everyone. There are at least three kinds of aloneness. Our concern here is the aloneness that comes with our inherited separation; biological separation is the uniqueness of being human. Each person is wrapped in a private package to live alone. God puts everyone in a container by himself and seals him in, to live his separate life.

While living in the world, each of us is shut up to his own inner world; we experience life in a state of separation from every other life. This separate life means that we are born to aloneness. Our inherited endowment makes us separate from every other person and from his environment. And the aloneness of our separation is both the burden and greatness of being human.

Yet there is a small part of life that we must share with others. We share our appearances. Others see our physical features, such as color of hair and eyes, height, and weight. By our words, we communicate feelings and experiences to other people. We open windows to our inner worlds by telling how we feel and by relating our experiences. This sharing is determined by the desire, or ego strength of individuals.

There are other ways we communicate a part of our lives to the outside world. By a false smile or hollow laugh we often reveal inner distress. Outward mirth can be an effort to cloak hidden sorrow. Superficial laughter may ripple over the surface of life as we try to hide the sullen darkness lying beneath. Yet great soul agonies cannot be laughed away; to the sensitive soul is indicated trouble deep in life. In the words of Shelley, "Our sincerest laughter with some pain is fraught."

The tone of voice, gesture of the hand, and expression of the face can also open up a little of the inner world that one is unwilling or unable to share. Even so, only a fragment of life is seen. A human life is somewhat like a pond: we see the bubbles and ripples come to the surface but know little of what is beneath the water. In the midst of millions of people, one lives mostly alone. Others do not see our silent selves. The common lot of human beings is that each one lives apart from any other person.

■ *Human aloneness is a part of our awareness.* A human is not only alone but also aware of being alone. The awareness of self-apartness from everybody and everything gives the set to life. Even though a person inherits aloneness and the potential for awareness of a separate existence, awareness of a separate existence is acquired as he develops from infancy. A human comes to perceive himself as separate and different from everything and everybody. This perception emerges from physical, mental, and emotional growth.

Awareness begins to form in infancy as a child slowly learns to distinguish his body from his environment. He learns from such activities as pullng his hair, twisting his toes, poking his finger in his eyes, and then crying because of the pain. Interaction with others makes him perceive himself as similar but different from others.

With self-awareness comes the knowledge that one is a certain kind of person, different from everything and everybody. Nobody else in the entire world is the same as he, a fact documented by his fingerprints. Consequently, self-awareness is awareness of a separate and different existence.

■ *Human aloneness is more than some people can bear.* Why does a person kill himself? Suicide is an effort to end a separate and permanent life, to blow out one's own life light. Thus it is also rooted in human aloneness, and aloneness is another condition inherited by every person. Every man, woman, and child is a solitary self.

Humans face a threefold problem because of their awareness of inherited aloneness. The problem emerges as loneliness, desire to escape existence, or fear of nonexistence. It is the desire to escape existence that helps bring a person to the suicide crisis. And it is this desire that roots the problem of suicide in human aloneness. The basic problem of the suicidal person is his inability to cope with his separate existence. He cannot live with the kind of person he has become. He is either unable or unwilling to assume responsibility for living his life. Therefore, the fundamental issue in dealing with suicide is life, not death!

A woman I will call Martha is an excellent example of a person who mastered human aloneness. Though life had not been easy for her, she had overcome life's obstacles to live a worthwhile life. She could have given up the struggle and withdrawn into a shell of aloneness. Her trials and troubles could have made her want to escape her separate existence. Her husband had died, leaving her to live by herself. Along with her aloneness, her children had been a disappointment to her. Also she was in constant pain because of an illness.

One day when she was leaving her physician's office, the doctor expressed sympathy for her because she had to "live alone." In a firm voice, Martha said: "Doctor, I have had many sorrowful experiences; my body is always in pain; my children have been a great disappointment to me. I do miss my husband so very much, but I do not live all alone." Then, with a sweet smile on her face she uttered in a soft voice: "I am never alone; Jesus is always with me."

This little woman's testimony was not a cover-up. It was not a denial of reality. It was not a facade—a smile on her face and a cry in her heart. Her words were a witness to the presence of Jesus Christ in her life. While God had not delivered her from her afflictions, He was with her in her afflictions. God's presence filled her life with grace. His presence made her a sweet Christian who gave a dynamic witness of His presence. Martha, like hundreds of other struggling people, has found the secret to resolving human aloneness.

Here, we need to focus on the aloneness of suicidal people. People in a suicide struggle fear existence more than they fear nonexistence; they are unable to handle a separate and permanent life. Suicide crisis is rooted in human aloneness.

Why does a person kill himself? He takes his life because he feels out of place in the world. This world is not a home for his life; therefore, he attempts to destroy his life. He believes that he has become a misfit and stranger. His separate life has become a confused entanglement with his environment and other people. The person in the suicide crisis sees no solution, other than the destruction of his miserable life.

SUICIDE AN EFFORT TO KILL FEELINGS

Beth woke up feeling on top of the world. She jumped out of bed, and during her shower she sang happily. Both her mind and body tingled with anticipation of a wonderful day.

As Beth entered her office, she had the same bright and

cheerful spirit she felt while getting ready for work. Then one by one the other workers came to work, passing by her office on the way to their offices. First, Mr. Ray came by and asked: "Did you not sleep well last night? You look tired." Next, Sue stopped to chat a moment and said: "You look like you have a temperature." Later, when Janice came by she asked: "Are you all right? You look like you are not feeling well." After similar suggestions from two other workers, Beth was feeling terrible. Finally, she left work and went home for the day. She began the day feeling grand; she ended it feeling sick; she experienced the power of mind over matter.

Beth did not know until the next morning that the other workers had conspired to feed her negative thoughts (she had been playing tricks on them). Even though done in fun, they changed her feelings and ruined her day. Nevertheless, Beth learned a valuable lesson—one's feelings can make or break one's day. However, the lesson Beth learned has not been learned by those who are suicidal; they do not realize that, like a sponge, they continually soak up negative feelings from their environment.

Be that as it may, a suicidal person kills himself to blot out his feelings. He thinks that by ending his life he will end his feelings. For even though a suicide crisis has roots in human frailty and human aloneness, the person in a suicide crisis has acquired certain feelings. What are the feelings involved in suicide? For example, if someone puts a gun to his head to kill himself, what are the feelings that bring him to the desperation point? How does he feel at the time he takes his own life? There are usually three strong feelings that possess a person who attempts self-destruction.

These three feelings are all members of the same family—the Ness family. First, there is Use Less Ness. Don't let his fancy name fool you; he is an enemy of life. Next, there is Help Less Ness. He deceives many people because of his first name *Help*. Remember though, his middle name does the damage; he enjoys seeing people in despair. The third member of the trio is named Hope Less Ness. Many fine people have had this same first name—Hope. Also, hope is an important word in the Bible—faith, hope, love (1 Cor. 13:13).

But, Hope is an alias for this feeling. This feeling's first name does not fit with faith and love; his name fits with doubt and despair. The members of the Ness family are notorious emotional gangsters, dedicated to the destruction of life.

■ *Uselessness.* The setting is a small town square in Jacksonville, Alabama. The actor is Cecil Andrews, an unemployed roofer, who had called a local television station to tell what he was going to do. The audience is two cameramen from the television station. The drama is a man setting himself on fire. The response is a sick feeling by people who view this horrible scene in the spring of 1983.

Andrews asked the cameramen if they would like to see someone burn. He then poured lighter fluid on his jeans, stuck a lighted match to them, and became a human torch. He burned while video equipment recorded the ghastly sight.

When sensitive people viewed this drama of death unfolding, in addition to the question of why the TV cameramen did nothing to stop him, they must have asked: "What feeling motivates a person to set himself on fire?" Of course, nobody can know the feelings of another person, especially a person who burns himself. While watching this tragedy, though, we can guess about his feelings; and speculation suggests a strong feeling of uselessness was present at the time he burned himself.

Millions of Americans experience a pervasive feeling of uselessness; they find life meaningless, empty, and miserable. They have no values for which to live; nothing seems worthwhile. As they have no stars on which to hang their lives, they are bored with life; they have no goals for which to strive. They flounder around in a void; they stew in their own misery.

A suicidal person feels good for nothing, that his life has no useful purpose. He feels that the world would be better off without him. He has tried and failed; life is too much for him; he is of no use to himself or others. His feeling of uselessness deprives him of the feedback needed for his own survival. A useful life has a feedback which enriches itself; by doing something for others, I do something for myself.

This feeling of uselessness brings the person in a suicide

crisis to a state of despair. In his despair, his feeling that life is useless increases to make him more and more inclined to end his life. A person in such a state of despair has become a victim of his own feeling of uselessness.

"My biggest problem is myself." The soft-spoken man seated in my office buried his face in his hands. I see many troubled people, but I rarely meet such honesty. Think of being able to recognize such a truth. How many people are willing to acknowledge it? "My biggest problem is myself!"

In a voice so low it could hardly be heard, the man continued: "Things became all fouled up, but it is I who am in the middle of them." He rose from his chair and walked to the window; there he stood silent for a few moments. When he spoke again, his trembling voice revealed pain far greater than his whispered words could express. "I create my own problems."

Nervously, as he stood silent he drummed on the windowpane. I respected his silence; I knew that he knew that I was with him, because we had already walked together in a long examination of a life dogged by failure. I knew that as he stared out the window, he looked beyond the rain that fell to make this Wednesday a dreary day—far beyond, to the unwritten record of his dreary life. "I create my own problems." With these words, he had reached a moment of insight obtained by few people.

This man had risen far above the level most people stay on, that of placing blame for failure on his neighbor, on his work, on his family, on his friends, or even on his enemies. He had reached the level where he put the blame squarely on himself, the level of personal responsibility.

His responsibility for personal failure came when he recognized that a part of his own self had unconsciously fought against success. He came to realize that he had become a victim of his feeling of uselessness. In his state of despair, he felt that death was better than his "useless life." While in his despair, this man believed that the only way to get rid of his feeling was to get rid of himself.

Even though not all people are plagued by failure, and not all who experience failure want to escape its pain by dying, most of us feel there are times when self defeats self. In our honest moments, almost all of us realize that we have internal problems of one sort or another that work to defeat us at one time or another. And the truth is that people have more trouble with themselves than with their neighbors.

The greatest battles of earth are fought not on the battle-field of war, but within the soul. It is within the soul of each individual person that the destructive elements of our lives cause constant conflict, sometimes unconsciously, sometimes overtly, a war sometimes so fierce that existence becomes a terrible burden, life a struggle wholly lacking in joy. For a person in a suicide crisis, these feelings, especially *uselessness*, are intense to the point of despair. One is so overcome by this feeling that he chooses to end his life.

■ *Helplessness.* On January 26, 1985, thirteen days before a suicide clause expired in his insurance policy, Frederick D. Holiday shot himself. As one viewed his life, he would think that this first black superintendent of Cleveland schools had many good things going for him. However, his suicide note revealed his feeling of helplessness, caused by the "petty politics" facing him in his position. Even though he was well qualified to handle his position, his helpless feeling prevented him from dealing with the "petty politics." Consequently, one day in early 1985 he killed himself rather than face them.

In addition to a feeling of uselessness, this feeling of helplessness is often found in a potential suicide. Being aware of his separate existence, the individual feels that life is more than he can handle. Though he is responsible for his life, he feels that his life has overcome him. He is ready to give up, because he feels helpless to cope with his own life. He knows that things are wrong in his life, but feels helpless to do anything about them. He is helpless to change the emotional pain.

Through the years many people appreciated the spunk of North Carolina Republican Senator John East. Despite the fact his legs had been paralyzed since 1955, he established himself as an outstanding senator. Also he had achieved in other work, such as teaching political science at East Carolina University in Greenville, North Carolina, and being a champion of the right to life. Nevertheless, in July 1986 he used automobile exhaust fumes to snuff out his own life. Even though he overcame the paralysis of his legs, evidently he felt helpless to do anything about his other physical problems—hypothyroidism and urinary problems; his depression was more than he could bear.

A suicidal person obviously feels helpless to change his miserable life. Along with his other feelings, this results in a suicide crisis. A person who has attempted suicide may make a remark such as: "I felt that I could not do anything else to ease the pain, but I could kill myself."

■ *Hopelessness.* Along with the feelings of uselessness and helplessness, there's the feelings of hopelessness, and this hopeless feeling appears to be the strongest feeling in driving a person to suicide. A feeling of hopelessness in people thinking of killing themselves has been observed to be the greatest predictor of them committing the act. The results of a study of patients hospitalized for contemplating suicide, conducted at University of Pennsylvania School of Medicine, supports this observation (*New York Times*, February 10, 1985).

When a feeling of hopelessness overcomes a suicidal person, all expectation on his part of any solution to his predicament has vanished. He feels that he is in an impossible situation with no way out; he feels beyond hope. The person who resorts to suicide sees no light at the end of his mental and emotional tunnel. He is blind to any solution for his pain, other than suicide. The hopelessness that permeates the lives of many people leaves them on a dead-end street, in mental and emotional pain.

Many years ago I saw a cartoon that depicted dramatically the feeling of so many people in a suicide crisis. A man with a paint brush in his hand stood in the far corner of a room away from the door. No wonder he had a hopeless expression on his face as he viewed his predicament. For he had started at the door, painting the floor, and had painted himself into a corner. The caption of the cartoon read: "No way out."

Millions in this land feel there is no way out of their predicament; they have ended in an inescapable corner of confusion, misery, or disappointment. Some stand without hope in an unbearable work situation. Others are paralyzed by hopeless family entanglements. Many live day after day with weak, frail, sickly bodies with no hope of relief from pain. Still others are pulled apart by unrelenting conflicts that appear insoluble. Far too many live with a past that refuses to stay in the past. Multitudes stew in hopelessness because of defeated plans and unobtainable goals; the sense of futility of life in general overwhelms them. People in suicide crises ask: "Is there no way out? Is there no answer? Is there no hope?"

When a Christian views the present American scene for a concerned look at the suicide epidemic, he realizes that millions of Americans have a feeling of hopelessness, because they are in a hopeless condition; seemingly, the only way out would be a miracle. Many are in a hopeless condition, because they have placed their hope in gods. When people serve gods, whether of their making or choosing matters not, they receive the help and hope these gods can give. The god of status gives power that can disappear overnight. The god of pleasure gives only fleeting satisfaction. The god of popularity gives fruits that spoil with time. The god of achievement gives only a sense of accomplishment. But believe me, when the testing time comes, the gods of earth will fail.

While standing in Boot Hill Graveyard on the edge of Tombstone, Arizona, I became absorbed in the history of this unusual place. For years after silver was discovered under these hills in 1877, Tombstone was a bloody and ruthless territory. For most citizens silver became a territorial god, and allegiance to this god resulted in death for many people. As I thought back to my childhood, I recalled the wild tales of Boot Hill Graveyard. In those years, reading the wild tales of the West, I thought of Tombstone as Dead Man's Land.

As an adult, thinking back on the early history of this place, I read the inscriptions on the tombstones; most of them tell how the people died. While reading the inscriptions—*shot, hanged, killed, lynched*—I did not expect to find the word suicide. I speculated that even if a person had been suicidal, somebody would have killed him before he could kill himself. Then suddenly I saw tombstones with "Suicide" written on them.

Surprised, I spent several minutes pondering why anybody would have killed himself in the early days of Tombstone. Finally, I concluded that worship of a silver god that crumbled resulted in such hopelessness that some people killed themselves before somebody else could kill them. For when a person worships a god instead of the true God, his life has very little permanent hope.

Therefore, it is not the degree of the predicament but the nature of the god that determines hopelessness or hopefulness. If one's hope is in a god, dark and lonely is the future. Unless one can look beyond the dark clouds of human programs and activities, permanent hope is not possible. Moreover, the past becomes a haunted house from which ghosts constantly visit the present. The present is filled with despondency and despair. The future offers a sense of futility and baseless existence.

However, whether the feeling of hopelessness is grounded in a realistic hopeless condition, or whether the feeling is groundless, it is nevertheless quite real to the suicidal person. And, the combination of a feeling of uselessness, helplessness, and hopelessness moves a person to despair.

Thus overcome with despair, he is struggling with a suicide crisis, and in danger of taking his own life. His belief that the only way to kill his feelings is to kill himself moves him toward suicide. When his feelings become painful enough, he will attempt to kill himself. Therefore, one reason a person kills himself is directly related to his feelings.

FACTORS IN SUICIDE

The chameleon, a lizard with the ability to change its color, is an interesting creature, especially for boys and girls. One day Marvin, an active ten-year-old boy, was playing with one. He placed a chameleon on green and it became green. When he placed it on red, it became red. In his experiment he put the lizard on one color after another and saw it take on its immediate environment.

Finally, remembering that his mother had a piece of multicolored cloth in the house, he wondered what it would do to the lizard. Being a boy who put feet on his ideas, he rushed into the house and got the checkered cloth; it was red, blue, and yellow. When he put the little lizard on the multicolored piece of cloth, it burst wide open trying to become all the colors at one time. The lizard's physical makeup—what it had become, and its world—where it had to survive, placed it in an impossible situation. It exploded!

Of course, this is only a tale, but it illustrates the predicament of many people. People generally have the ability to adapt to their environment, but sometimes they are unable to cope when their environment makes excessive demands on them. Having little self-identity, and trying to adjust to their environment, they burst wide open—a suicide crisis. What they have become, and where they have to survive, result in an emotional explosion; and sometimes there is a physical explosion—suicide.

Now, moving on from the three feelings that overwhelm a person who tries to take his own life, what are the suicide factors of attempted suicide? That is, what causes a person to snuff out his life? Why would a person take himself out of this world?

A search for an answer to these questions leads to factors inside and outside the suicidal person. A person in a suicide crisis has a storm raging in his inner world and in his outer world. The factors causing the inner storm are predisposing factors. The predisposing factors cause one to be predisposed to suicide; he is capable of killing himself. The factors causing the outer storm are called precipitating factors; they trigger suicide in the person who is already predisposed to it.

■ *Predisposing factors.* The predisposing factors have to do with the kind of person one has become. If a person wakes someone up in the middle of the night to tell him that he has a gun to his head and plans to pull the trigger, he did not begin his life at midnight; he has lived his life from the time he was a tiny baby until that midnight moment. He has become the person who now wants to kill himself. His self-image and weak survival need make him a person who chooses to face death rather than face life. Suicide is his way of handling the stress of his existence. He handles stress in this way because of the person he has become; this is the set of his life.

Many factors, along with the feelings mentioned above, result in a person who is inclined toward self-harm. If one's survival need is not strong enough to counteract the fear of existence, then suicide is more probable. Everyone has, no doubt, seen people with a weak survival need who "have no will to live." However, this set of life does not mean that the person will kill himself, because there are other factors in suicide.

■ *Precipitating factors.* The other factors, the precipitating factors, trigger off the suicide crisis. When a person is predisposed to suicide, and then experiences a precipitating factor, a suicide crisis results. "What then," you ask, "are the factors that trigger a suicide crisis?"

There are many possible factors. A special season or time of year, a personal loss, or any stressful situation may trigger off a suicide crisis. A holiday, such as Christmas, is especially rough for a person who is predisposed to self-murder. A birthday, anniversary, or other special time that brings back memories often causes problems for the person who is predisposed to suicide.

Any personal loss in the life of a person may trigger thoughts of suicide. For example, a loss such as the death of a loved one, a divorce, poor health, or a low academic standing in school often help to create a dangerous situation and push a person into suicide. Even a desire to get even with others by making them feel sorry, is often a precipitating factor. Let's focus on a few examples of factors which sometimes trigger suicide.

■ *A desire to make someone else hurt and get even may trigger suicide.* Tom and his wife had been having serious difficulties in their marriage for several weeks. She had told him that she no longer loved him and was in love with another man; so Tom wanted to hurt her as she had hurt him. He told her: "I can't keep you, but I can leave you with just a little of the pain which you have caused me." His wife did not suspect that he meant to do what he did; she did not recognize the subtle suicide threat. While they were sitting in the den watching television, he put his pistol to his head and shot himself.

■ *A low grade in school may cause a teenager to attempt suicide.* Jean's suicide crisis was triggered by a D in geometry. Her good grades were the only way she had of getting the attention and approval of her parents. When she realized that she had lost this way of getting approval by making a D in geometry, she could not handle her feelings of failure. Consequently, she entered a suicide crisis, and eventually made a serious attempt to end her life; she swallowed 100 Sudafed tablets and nearly died.

Even though Jean's parents had ignored her cries for help and several superficial attempts at suicide, she was blessed by having an alert school counselor. Then, when the counselor referred her to a school psychologist, he knew what to do, and how to get help for her. Thus, when she made the serious attempt to kill herself, she was in a medical facility, where she received emergency help to prevent her from dying.

While getting help, this young lady learned to survive with her troubled life. Eventually she coped enough to give her suicidal testimony to other people, and helped others while helping herself. She shared her suicidal struggles, enabling audiences to gain insight into the life of a person struggling with self-murder. Her suicidal testimony helped her by giving to her some of the attention she needs so much.

Jean's experience is an excellent example of a person whose life was predisposed to suicide, permitting a precipitating factor, the low grade in geometry, to trigger her crisis. Notwithstanding that much of her suicidal behavior appeared to be to get attention, if medical help had not been so close by when she made her serious attempt, she would have succeeded in killing herself.

Many adolescents have trouble with stress that most adults would consider insignificant. For example, a breakup with a boy or girl will sometimes cause an adolescent to make an attempt at self-destruction. Also, for some strange reason teenagers seem to be set off to kill themselves by hearing about others who have committed suicide.

■ *Thus another factor, publicity about suicides, is believed to precipitate suicide, and has recently been very much in the news.* Psychiatrists at Columbia University College of Physicians and Surgeons reported information which suggests that the media is responsible for increase in attempted suicide, and in increase of suicide. Their report indicates that there was a jump in suicides after the showing of each of the made-for-TV fictional films shown in 1984-85. These movies were intended to alert the viewing public to suicide, to the need for cooperation with schools in suicide prevention, and to encourage suicidal people to get help, but the motive did not prevent the negative impact on teenagers. A number of teen suicides followed. A statistically significant increase in teenage suicide after national coverage of news or feature stories about suicide was also reported by researchers at the University of California at San Diego.

It is helpful for a concerned person to know that any stressful event or situation may act as a factor to precipitate a suicide crisis in a person who is predisposed to suicide.

■ *Still another factor considered to cause suicide is drug abuse, including alcohol.* To relate drugs to the suicide epidemic is easy; to establish a cause-effect relationship between drugs and suicide is not always so easy. We need to consider at least four relationships of drugs to suicide.

First, we need to be cautious about making the generalization that drug abuse causes much of teenage suicide, because even though it appears that drugs caused the suicide, sometimes drugs are present but did not cause the act. Rather, in many cases drug abuse and suicide are caused from the same root factor. That is, the painful feelings which caused a person to be a drug abuser cause him to kill himself.

Therefore, when a person on drugs kills himself, it is not necessarily true that the drugs caused him to take his life. The same inability to cope with life moves the person to both drug abuse and suicide. The same desire to escape the hard reality of one's existence results in drug abuse and self-murder. In such cases there is not cause and effect between drug abuse and suicide, but there is cause-effect relationship between the two and the feelings which make a person want to get away from his struggle. In one case the person escapes life by mind altering drugs; in the other case he escapes life by killing himself.

Second, there are times when certain drugs bring to the surface of one's mind homicide or suicide. When this happens, drug abuse ignites the thought of harming somebody else or one's self. Thus under the influence of drugs, a person may either kill another person or kill himself. When a person commits either of these acts under the influence of drugs, there is certainly a cause-and-effect relationship between drugs and suicide, or homicide.

Doris was an example of high-level teenage living; she was an A student, and the pride of her teachers and parents. Furthermore, her reputation and activity spread beyond the boundaries of her home and school; she was involved in community activities and was the organist for her church. Therefore when she lost control of herself and tried to attack her teachers, everybody who knew her was surprised and alarmed.

When Doris' mother related the above information to me before my first session with Doris, I was prepared for dealing with a girl with an unusual problem. However, when the well-mannered girl who reflected quality culture entered my office, it was hard to believe that she had attacked her teachers. Soon though, her story unfolded to reveal the cause of her abnormal behavior; it also revealed suicidal thoughts.

For months Doris had been taking painkillers which had been prescribed by her physician. Eventually it had brought to the surface homicidal and suicidal struggles. When the effects of this drug were out of her system, she did not experience any more abnormal behavior, and continued with her productive life. Nevertheless, this fine girl is an excellent example of drug abuse causing a homicidal and suicidal problem. If Doris had not got help, her life would have become a tragedy.

Third, drug abuse, especially alcohol, may cause a person's inhibitions to be let down, resulting in behavior which the person would control if he were not under its influence. Thus if a person is struggling with suicide, and then gets under the influence of drugs, his inhibitions could be quieted to result in self-inflicted death. When this happens to a person, drugs certainly cause him to kill himself.

Fourth, sometimes drugs cause a person to kill himself when he does not intend to end his life. If a person is under the influence of mind-altering drugs, his perceptual processes are changed. By perceptual processes, I mean the process whereby raw matter is changed to meaning. For example, a traffic light is not just a light; it is a red or green light. Another example is that of distance from a three-story window to the ground below; when one's perception of distance is impaired by drugs, the distance may appear to be three feet when it is actually thirty feet.

Consequently, there are drug abusers who kill themselves because they are under the influence of drugs. However, in certain cases the person had no intention of killing himself. In such cases it is correct to say that the drugs caused the person to kill himself; it is not correct to say that he intended to kill himself.

■ *Ignoring of one's cry for help may trigger suicide.* While Jack was in the United States military service, suicidal thoughts began to gnaw at him. Realizing that he had problems, he sought help, but nobody would listen. So he wrote a suicide note and killed himself:

> I want all my worldly goods to go to my father and mother. I am doing this for you; this is what you wanted.
> I think that you have been the greatest folks I know.
> I still say that there is something wrong with me, but I always was a hard guy to get along with. It's better this way.
> I could say more about myself, but I don't think anybody would listen to my story.
> God bless both of you and all the kids.

This young man's suicide note reflects two important facts about his situation: his thinking was confused and his cries for help were ignored.

■ *Fear of criminal exposure and loss of reputation may trigger suicide.* When the 12-year-old daughter of an army officer found him hanging by a rope from a bannister, it must have been a traumatic experience for her. Only two weeks before, this 45-year-old man had resigned from a very successful position at an army arsenal. He had lived a productive life and given worthwhile service to the United States Army. Now, found by his own child, he lay dead by self-inflicted wounds.

Under pressure and fear of public exposure for misdeeds, he preferred death to life. With him, as with many before and after him, loss of reputation was more than he wanted to bear. The weight of what he was facing triggered suicide.

■ *A breakup with a lover may trigger suicide, especially in a teenager.* Spring was exploding in every aspect of nature. The rays of the sun beamed down on blooming flowers. Birds fluttered through the trees singing their melodious sonnets. Budding trees spoke the unique language of springtime. People hurried about involved in their daily chores, exclaiming: "Spring is sprung!" As the breeze flowed gently to tickle the faces of children playing in the park, all appeared to be well with the inhabitants of the small town. But all was not well; two teenagers struggled with their lives.

Mildred, a pretty sixteen-year-old girl who had just broken up with her boyfriend, struggled with an important decision. She could not get Ted's parting words out of her mind: "I feel so alone when I am not with you. I had rather be dead than live without you." Mildred knew that Ted did not have any close friends; he lived a very lonely life, because he was not close to his family either. Because she believed that he might harm himself, she was very worried about him and wondered what she should do. Finally, she decided to talk with his mother and express her concern.

Meantime, alone in his room where he spent much of his time, Ted struggled with himself. Since his breakup with Mildred, he felt that his world had ended. He felt so alone that he wanted no longer to exist.

As Mildred walked up on the porch of Ted's home, she was so afraid of talking with his mother, a rather harsh person, that she was trembling, fearful of her reaction. Nevertheless, Mildred rang the doorbell, told his mother about her concern that he would harm himself, and returned to her home, relieved that Ted's mother had appreciated her concern for Ted.

Later, Mildred heard what happened. After she left Ted's home, his mother went immediately to his room, where she found Ted lying on the floor, unconscious from an overdose of pills. He had gotten his teddy bear out of the closet where it had been since he was a child, and was holding it in his arms; he was trying to escape his aloneness. Since Ted was already predisposed to self-harm, his breakup with Mildred triggered suicide.

At a hospital, doctors and nurses pulled him back from the edge of death. He was rescued from suicide because someone recognized the danger and cared enough to help. Even though afraid of Ted's mother, Mildred did what she could to get help for him. If she had not responded to his talk of suicide as she did, when she did, Ted's story would be tragically different.

SUICIDE: A COMBINATION OF FACTORS

When I was a boy growing up in the country, catching wild rabbits was a pleasant experience. Most boys knew how to build a box or trap for catching them. These traps give an excellent illustration of the predisposing and precipitating factors in suicide.

A rabbit box has a door at the entrance connected to a trigger inside the box. When the box is set, a piece of apple is placed back behind the trigger. The wild rabbit would enter the front of the box, move toward the back to get the apple, and in so doing trip the trigger. The door would drop shut, trapping the rabbit inside. Get the picture. The rabbit box was already set—predisposed, when the rabbit, the precipitating factor, triggered the set box. The suicidal person is set—predisposed, when the stress factor triggers off the crisis.

Even though one has become the kind of person who is predisposed to suicide, and experiences stress in his life, there are two things which one needs to remember. A person with an inner suicide storm may never experience enough storm in his environment to cause a suicide crisis. He may have a low self-image and a weak survival need, but not experience enough stress from his outer world to cause him to attempt to take his life. On the other hand, a person predisposed to suicide may be triggered into attempted suicide by what appears to be a small amount of stress.

SUMMARY

In summary, why then does a person kill himself? One reason is to try to escape life—human frailty and human aloneness. He wants to bring his life to an end; he views death as the only way to do this; death is a way of escape. Because he chooses death in preference to life, death becomes an avenue of escape from an unbearable life.

A second reason a person kills himself is to ease his emotional pain. Due to his feeling of uselessness, helplessness, and hopelessness, the suicidal person is in a state of despair. He perceives suicide as the only way to ease this pain. Therefore, in one sense, suicide is an effort to kill the feelings and relieve the agonizing distress.

A third reason a person kills himself is to quiet his inner

storm and resolve his outer conflicts. Certain factors within himself make him predisposed to suicide. He has fallen out of love with life; he either has no desire to live or feels his life is not worth living. Then something in his external world connects with his internal world to set off a crisis. The outer stress triggers his inner turmoil to move him toward death. The likelihood that his inner storm helped to develop the conflicts in his environment, does not weaken the influence of the stress upon his inner world.

Remember though, a person may be inclined to suicide, and not have any definite trouble until something happens to trip the trigger. A special holiday, such as Christmas, may cause a lonely person to have thoughts of harming himself; more people kill themselves during the Christmas season than at any other time. Anyone who has a relative or friend with suicidal tendencies should see that the person has special support on holidays. Similarly, a person with suicidal tendencies who suffers the loss of a job needs special help through the crisis.

Teenagers may attempt suicide because of failing a course in school, or a broken "puppy-love" relationship. Special help and support should be given to any person who is predisposed to suicide and experiencing excessive stress.

This section should close with a caution: Almost any person could be troubled with thoughts of suicide, if his defense mechanism is broken down by stress. Please don't make a mistake which so many people make when a relative or friend is under great stress. So often, significant people in the person's life say: "He is strong enough to handle it." He may well handle it by killing himself.

5 HOW TO KEEP A PERSON FROM TAKING HIS LIFE— GENERAL SUGGESTIONS

A certain man attended church every Sunday but never applied the pastor's sermon to himself. Each week when the pastor greeted him at the door, he would say, "You sure told them about it today." Finally, the pastor found his opportunity to preach a sermon just to this man. During a bad snowstorm only the man came to church. The pastor sang a hymn, prayed, and then preached a sermon to the man who never considered that the sermon was for him.

Afterward, the pastor was thinking, "I told you about it this morning." However, when the pastor greeted the man, he said, "That was a good sermon, pastor; if they had been here, you would really have told them about it today."

We all too often tend to pass on to somebody else the counsel meant for us. The suggestions in this chapter are life-or-death matters, and should not be thought of as for some other reader. All of us need to be ready to help a person struggling with thoughts of suicide.

On one bright Monday morning a certain pastor entered his church study, thankful for a peaceful day. While thinking about the work he would do that day, he received a call from a frantic member of his congregation. Her grandson, 500 miles away in another state, had just told her in a phone call that he was going to jump off a bridge—a *blue* bridge, he said. The grandmother was hysterical.

The pastor responded in a commendable way. He could have told the grandmother, "Don't worry; he won't really jump." Or he could have told her that he could only pray about the crisis. He did pray, but he also called the sheriff's office in the boy's county. Sure enough, the person who received his call knew about the blue bridge and dispatched an officer to the scene. A suicide was prevented because a concerned grandmother called her pastor, and he knew how to get help.

Suicide is a leading cause of death in the United States, and it will eventually touch the lives of most of us. We can put our heads in the sand and ignore it. We can try to shift the problem to somebody else. Or we can recognize suicide as a problem and make a sensible approach to solving it. If we do accept this problem as our problem, one by one we must learn how to help a suicidal person. So now let us focus on this great need and examine some approaches and techniques for preventing suicide.

SEEK PERSONAL GROWTH

You, at some time in your life, will likely be involved with someone who attempts suicide. You may receive a cry for help from a person in the throes of a suicide crisis. Your phone could ring and you could answer to hear a voice say, "I would be better off dead than alive." Or you could receive a call from a friend or neighbor pleading for help to aid someone else bent on suicide. How would you respond to such cries?

If you should face someone struggling with suicide, would you have enough emotional strength to help the person, or would you fall apart? Possibly you need to grow as a person to increase your emotional health. All of us need to experience both emotional and spiritual growth as we move along in life. Since it is possible for our relationship with a suicidal person to either help or harm, we need to consider both a caution and a challenge.

■ *A caution.* If we want to do our best in preventing suicide, we need emotional strength to interact with a person in a healthful way. To help another person, one in a life-or-death crisis, we need to be in control of our own lives. We need an inner sense of security and peace. We need to overcome our own sense of aloneness. We need the emotional strength to meet and master the obstacles we face in our daily living. So why not take a look at number one, yourself? It may be painful, but it is necessary.

Our feelings are important, because if we were to receive

a call from someone struggling with suicide, feelings could determine our response. If we were to receive such a crisis call, and a storm was raging inside of us, our inner storm would color our interpretation of the other person's problem. We would project our inner turmoil to the person in the suicide crisis. We would likely interpret his situation based on our feelings rather than on his feelings. And, by so doing we could do harm while trying to help.

A husband who tried to get help for his wife illustrates how one's own inner turmoil may color his interpretation of another person's problem. This man believed that his wife needed psychological or psychiatric help; yet it did not matter how much he tried, she would not go for help. Finally, he decided that if she would not go for help, he would bring the help to her. So he found a psychologist who agreed to make a house call.

During the interview, the psychologist asked the man's wife, "Do you ever see any pink elephants in the room?" She replied, "No, sir, I do not." Immediately the man took the psychologist into another room and said, "See, it's like I told you; she is crazy." "What do you mean?" the psychologist asked. The husband then whispered in his ear, "She said there are no pink elephants in the room, and the room is full of pink elephants."

Granted, this illustration is humorous and perhaps far-fetched, but we must be careful while trying to deal with the storm inside the person in the suicide crisis, when the storm is out of control inside of us. I do not mean that emotional problems will keep you from helping a person who is bothered by suicidal thoughts. I do mean you must be careful how you help. If you think that your problems will increase the person's problem, you may want to avoid direct contact with the person. Nevertheless, you can still help a person by getting help for him. And by so doing you will save the person's life.

This caution does not mean that people with problems cannot help a suicidal person. If this were true, none of us would be able to help a person in despair. All of us have problems. The caution stresses that people with certain problems make matters worse for a person in a suicide struggle. When this happens, we can help in ways other than interacting with the suicidal person. But when we have emotional strength to help a suicidal person, let us get involved and help.

■ *A challenge.* Most of us who work with troubled people need to experience emotional growth to be more effective in helping others.

Does this mean we should wait for emotional growth before helping others? No! Instead, we should continue to help others while we seek emotional growth. If we can experience self-improvement, let us do so and become better qualified to help suicidal people. Some of us are able to use self-help techniques for emotional growth; other people will need help from someone else.

Help for emotional growth can be anywhere from a shallow look at one's self to indepth analysis. Thus self-help does not lose sight of, or seek to be a substitute for psychological or psychiatric treatment by a qualified professional. When people need such treatment, they should get it. The wise person will certainly make use of available mental health resources when he needs them. Nonetheless, when a person knows what is preventing him from being an emotionally healthy person, and he has the strength to deal with it without special help, he should do so.

Self-help techniques are for the average person who, it is assumed, has enough emotional strength to face himself. They offer growth for those who are big enough, or enough at ease with themselves, to come to grips with their own lives. They offer freedom for growth to those who are able to use available resources to free themselves from emotional bondage.

So where does this leave most of us? If we want to use self-help techniques for emotional growth, we can find such teaching in self-improvement books. However, the following steps can lead to emotional growth.

■ *Step 1: Open your life to spiritual resources.* It is a mistake to assume that the Christian experience is an automatic and miraculous removal of all our poor habits of thinking and acting. True, our relationship with God offers help for victorious living; yet to assume the attitude of many professed Christians is absurd; namely, that God will take all the quirks out of one's personality without any personal effort.

A more realistic and correct view is that our Christian

experience gives identity as children of God, gives direction to life, and gives a new power for life. Becoming a Christian does not of itself solve all of our problems, but rather relates us to our Heavenly Father who understands us and our problems. And certainly there is no reason why we should not acknowledge and use the blessings of our new life. The promises of God offer help for our problems. We can claim these promises and still avoid a distorted concept of God which sees Him as a glorified wrecker whose sole work is to pull us out of self-made ditches.

The enjoyment of Christian resources and blessings is much different from the approach that takes God to be a narcotic for human ailments. Hope and strength come as a result of our relationship with God. Our walk with Him, though, is not to obtain the fruit from His hand, but to enjoy His fellowship: true Christian experience is at the core of our existence, not something that we turn on and off at our pleasure and for our profit.

Christian experience is not something to use, but a life to live. Rather than expect that our troubles always be removed, we expect God to be with us in our troubles. Thus we claim the fellowship, guidance, and power of our new life in our efforts to become emotionally healthy, rather than expecting removal of all our personality problems. We enjoy the resources which God has given: prayer, Bible study, and fellowship. And, as we enjoy our relationship with the Lord, we experience personal growth.

■ *Step 2: Read good self-improvement books.* Many excellent books have been written for people who want to improve themselves. On the other hand, many self-help books are valueless. If in doubt about a book, inquire about it from others; check out the author. When reading self-help books, use the common sense one uses when eating fish: eat the meat and discard the bones.

■ *Step 3: Share your life with others.* There are many lonely people who need someone to share their lives. Give of yourself to sick people; visit people who are shut-ins because of age or illness; open your heart to people who are experiencing suffering or trouble. As you share your life, it radiates emotional healing to others.

■ *Step 4: Express love.* Many love-starved hearts are reaching out for affection. True Christian love breaks down the barriers which separate one person from another. While superficial words of affection should be shunned, honest expressions of love can heal a multitude of hurts. When we speak words of love with sincerity and meaning, we are experiencing emotional and spiritual growth.

While visiting the members of the Sunday School class she taught, April learned that a neighbor of a class member was in the hospital with a self-inflicted injury. Even though she knew little about attempted suicide, April felt a desire to visit the young woman. The young teacher expressed a desire to visit the victim, and the class member volunteered to accompany her to the hospital.

However, as the two young women approached the hospital room of the injured woman, fear gripped them. "What will we say to her?" April asked, turning to her friend. The member of April's Sunday School class had learned well the lessons that they had been studying in their class. "I know," she said, "we can just tell her that we love her and want to help her."

These two women not only spoke words of love but also "put feet" to their love in a Christlike manner. They continued to visit her in the hospital and won her to the Lord; she is now an active member of their Sunday School class, and lives a meaningful life.

We develop our love by loving and being loved; and by so doing, we become emotionally healthy agents to help cure the ills of a suffering people. We become people who can empathize with someone in a suicide crisis. When a person in a suicide crisis recognizes this special love, he is able to respond and thereby become receptive to help.

Self-help techniques are not for every person. One should by no means engage in morbid examination that produces less self-control, withdrawal from others, or a feeling of uselessness, helplessness, or hopelessness. If one finds that he is becoming preoccupied with his feelings, depressed, disorganized, or less effective in his relationships and environment, he should seek help from a qualified counselor.

GETTING HELP FROM OTHERS

When a Christian recognizes that he needs help, what action can he take? Even though many people become disappointed in their search, help is available. But caution is advised in choosing outside help. I suggest the following resources in making a wise choice.

■ *A therapy or interaction group.* The group may consist of six or eight people under the care of a trained counselor or therapist. The nonthreatening atmosphere enables one to feel safe to undertake an examination of life. The protective and supportive give-and-take of participants permits interaction that frees one from the need to hide feelings and thoughts.

Thus a participant can experience freedom that will enable him to recognize, accept, and discuss his most intimate problems. Because he doesn't fear rejection, dealing within the therapy group with the alien elements of his own life will be easier. Acceptance by the group helps each member to accept himself and others.

Being a member of a therapy group puts one in a mental and emotional atmosphere in which he can experience self-understanding. When other members admit their faults and weaknesses, a participant will be inclined to admit his. The feeling of belonging gives ego strength to bear the interpretation the group makes of his life. Because the group supports him in his effort at self-understanding, he is even strong enough to endure confrontation by the group, when seeking to evade or cover up his weakness or faulty response pattern.

The group too should always be led by a therapist or counselor trained in human behavior, group dynamics, and counseling techniques, one capable of giving support, encouragement, interpretation, clarification, and guidance, and setting an atmosphere for confrontation. Churches would do well to make this kind of resource available to troubled people.

Before becoming involved in a group, one should know three things: the training and character of the group leader, the purpose of the group counseling, and the basis for selection of group members. Without careful checking, one could join group members with whom he has nothing in common, or become involved in a cult group and be brainwashed.

■ *Pastoral counseling.* If group therapy is not available, or is not the method of help one needs, pastoral counseling may help him. Many clergymen take clinical training in addition to their academic education. Such training enables a minister to gain a better understanding of himself and others, and counseling techniques, to relate Bible truth to human problems.

One is blessed indeed if he has such a pastor. A pastor can walk with a person as he examines his life. A skilled pastor can lend a listening ear while one talks out his negative feelings, his faults and failures, his desires and needs, his goals and values, his methods and madness. He can give acceptance, understanding, clarification, interpretation, and guidance as one seeks a realistic picture of himself in his world.

Trained pastors are qualified to deal with a variety of problems, including those related to marriage, family, and vocational matters. A pastor trained to counsel will know his own limitations; he will not try to be a "junior psychiatrist"; he will know when to refer a counselee to someone more qualified. Of course, every person has the responsibility of determining a pastor's character and qualifications. Furthermore, don't expect therapy sessions from a pastor.

■ *Individual counseling or psychotherapy.* When a Christian believes that he needs counseling or therapy on a deeper psychological level, I recommend a qualified psychologist or psychiatrist. In cases of severely emotionally disturbed people, I recommend a psychologist or psychiatrist as a must. As when choosing any resource for personal assistance, one should be cautious when choosing a psychologist or psychiatrist.

A qualified psychiatrist is a person who has studied medicine to earn a degree in medicine (M.D.), and has done additional training to become certified in psychiatry. However, these qualifications alone do not mean that the person will be a good counselor. If one plans to trust his life to a person in a counseling relationship, he should know, at least by reputation, something about the person's character. Also, he should know whether the psychiatrist does counseling; many psychiatrists are not counselors; they use other treatment for their patients.

A qualified psychologist is a person who has studied human behavior to earn a degree in human behavior

(Ph.D.), and may have done additional training to become certified in psychology. Still, such a person may not be a good counselor for two reasons: since there are several areas of psychology, a psychologist may not have training in counseling; also, the character of the psychologist may not recommend him as a good counselor.

However, the saying that all psychologists and psychiatrists are atheists is false; many of them are Christians, active in their churches. For the person in need of a counselor trained in human behavior, my advice is to take action and seek help without delay.

SEEK SUICIDE CLUES

Much excitement filled the air as students arrived at the junior college campus for the beginning of a new school year. Some of the excitement continued into orientation day as administrators and teachers bombarded students with information. However, the excitement changed to embarrassment and laughter as the college president was giving his annual instructions to the student body.

A professor, feeling that the auditorium was too warm, handed the building custodian a note. The custodian thought that the note was for the president and gave it to him. Thinking that the note was an announcement, the president read it aloud: "Turn off the hot air; it is making us sick."

Much of what we see and hear is misinterpreted; we fail to consider the real message. This all too often happens when a suicidal person signals that he is struggling with suicide. We misinterpret what he says or does; consequently, we fail to hear his cry for help.

I agree with the saying: "If God had intended that we talk twice as much as we listen, He would have given to us two mouths and one ear. But He didn't do that; He gave to us two ears and one mouth, because He intended for us to listen twice as much as we talk."

We may prevent a person from killing himself by hearing his cry for help; we need to love enough to listen. The person who wants to help suicidal people must learn the signs, clues, and warnings given by people in a suicide struggle. Someone struggling with suicide will give either verbal clues, covert behavioral clues, or both.

VERBAL CLUES

■ *Direct clues of suicidal pain.* Most people with thoughts of suicide will at sometime, to some person, verbalize clues of suicidal intentions. Someone with thoughts of self-destruction may make a remark such as, "My family would be better off without me." One remark often heard is, "You won't be seeing me around." Or, you may hear such talk as, "Life is not worth living"/"I would be better off dead"/"I am not good for anything"/"I am in the way." Even though some people say outright, "I am going to kill myself," many people struggling with suicide give subtle clues, such as talking about death or acting suddenly to make a will.

■ *"Another person" clues.* Some people talk about another person with suicidal tendencies, when, in fact, referring to themselves. This happened with a person employed in the building where I formerly worked. He told my secretary that he must see me because of an emergency. When I saw him, he told be about a friend who was about to kill himself. In time I realized he himself was the one losing control. He himself had purchased a gun, because he could not endure life. He was the person who would be better off dead. This man was crying for help for himself.

■ *Stress Clues.* As to the interpretation of verbal clues, it should be made in view of the stress factors. Talk of making a will by a healthy and happy person would be viewed differently from such talk by a person discouraged by poor health, or a person withdrawn or depressed. The meaning of what appears to be suicidal talk must be evaluated according to the emotional and mental state of the person, along with stress factors.

■ *Clues telegraphed by children.* Interpretation of what appears to be suicidal talk by children is even more complicated than it is with adults. Years ago parents paid little attention when a child said, "I am going to kill myself." Now, because so many children are killing themselves, it is dangerous for parents to ignore remarks that suggest their children are thinking of self-harm.

A child may get angry, or just want to have his way, and say, "I wish that I were dead." On the other hand, statistics of suicide by children suggest there may well be danger for a child who makes such a statement; he may harm himself. While a parent should not become hysterical, let the child manipulate him, or overreact with fear, one ought to give due concern to the child's talk of suicide.

BEHAVIORAL CLUES

As to behavioral clues, they are more complicated than verbal clues. Suppose that a member of your family buys a gun. Your response would, of course, be determined by what you know about the person. In any case, it would be unwise to overreact to the purchase. It could be that the family member intends to start hunting, or is afraid of someone breaking into the house.

Here again, you need to know the person. Because if that same person is under great stress, is agitated or depressed, or acts in a strange or suspicious manner, the purchase of a gun could have a different meaning, and action on your part may save the person from suicide.

A CASE HISTORY

There are many people who love a person in a suicide struggle and are willing to do anything to help, but either fail to recognize the danger or don't know what to do to help the person. Such was the case with the Christian woman who shares the following tragic story. She wants to alert others to warning signals to prevent them from making the mistake she made. Her experience reveals several verbal and nonverbal suicide clues. Learn from her experience with suicide:

When I went to work on this particular morning, little did I expect the pain and loss that would come before the end of the day. Everything seemed to be fine, and it was for about two hours, until a co-worker came to me on my coffee break and said she was going to take me home. When I noticed that she had my purse and jacket with her, I knew that she was not kidding. So I asked her why she was taking me home. All she would say was that I was needed at home. I could not understand her behavior, because being needed at home was not anything new for me; my mother had been in and out of the hospital for about a year, and I had been called home several times to see about her. Also, I could not understand why my co-worker wanted to drive me home. I had always driven home before when I was needed.

So I told my co-worker that my car was there and I could drive home. Another friend said: "Give me your keys because I am going to bring your car." It suddenly dawned on me that something tragic had happened. Still my friends would not tell me anything.

As we drove the two miles to my home, my mind was racing first to my mother, then to my son, and then to my brother. I knew that something terrible had happened to one of them, and I wondered which one it was. A short time after we left work, we met an ambulance; I then knew that it was not my son because he was not at home. This seemed the longest two miles I ever traveled. Finally we reached my home.

When we arrived at my house, the pastor's wife met me with the news that my brother had shot himself in the head. She told me that he was alive when the ambulance left with him for the hospital. She also told me that my pastor had gone with them to the hospital and would call as soon as he learned my brother's condition. They wanted me to stay at our home until the pastor called. In about thirty minutes he called to say that my brother had died a few minutes after he arrived at the emergency room.

If you have not been through the experience of losing a loved one by suicide, there is no way you can know the suffering that I experienced during the following hours. Over and over my mind was asking: "Why?" This question is still haunting me. Thoughts of things that had happened to him over the last ten years rushed into my thinking.

Looking back on this tragedy, I realize several things about my brother. If I had only recognized them before he killed himself, perhaps I could have prevented his death. Nothing I can do will now help him, but I hope to help somebody else.

Depression. Even though my brother did beautiful work and had great potential as a commercial artist, he could not apply his time and talent to his work. More and more he would not go in to work. At first it was a day or two at a time, but later he would be away from work for weeks. He did appear to be sick, yet he would not go to a doctor. He would stay in his room, only coming out to eat and go to the bathroom. At these times he was almost completely withdrawn from the family.

Things seemed to happen to my brother to make him feel more and more down in the dumps. Because he did not work to have income, he had to give up his automobile. His depression seemed to make things happen to him to cause him to be more depressed.

Because my brother would not go to the doctor and appeared to be sick, there were several times when I called the doctor to the house to examine him. I now realize that my brother was not physically ill but mentally ill. If the doctor knew this, he never mentioned it to us.

Verbal signals. I had heard my brother express a desire for death many times but thought it was just talk. I should have listened but did not. There were times when he would say: "I wish I could go to sleep and never wake up."

Once he took his dog and a rifle and went into the woods. We thought he had gone hunting. Several days later he said: "The day I went into the woods pretending to hunt, I planned to take my life, but could not do it when I got there." When I asked him why he had that desire, he said: "I have nothing to live for. The people I thought were my friends never come around to see me. I can't keep work to help support the home; I am just no good to anyone."

Even though I was shocked by hearing him express a desire to kill himself, I thought he really did not intend to do this; I thought that he probably felt sorry for himself and only wanted some sympathy. Now looking back, I realize that he was experiencing mental torture. I just wish that I could have known more about suicide back then, so that I could have done more to help him.

Drugs. Another problem for my brother was drugs. Somewhere along the line, I don't know when or where, he was introduced to amphetamines. Then too he was taking barbiturates. He would take the stimulates to keep him going, and then work day and night, trying to get his work finished. When he was completely exhausted, he would withdraw to his room, where he would stay for weeks, only coming out occasionally, for example, to eat. He seemed seriously sick, but made it very clear to the family that he did not want to be bothered. I always suspected that he was on other drugs, but did not know for sure.

In spite of the fact that he at times did some work, he never had any money. Along with this, there was a man who occasionally came to the house on a motorcycle to see my brother. He never came in the house, and I never knew the purpose of his visits. All of these things worried and puzzled me, but I did not know what to do.

Regret. In retrospect, I now know there were many complicated factors in my brother's life. The sadness of his childhood, his unpleasant experience in the military service, and his complicated love life, all made him a very complex person. My own stupidity about the signs I saw before his death still haunt me.

Our ray of hope. About ten weeks before he killed himself, he accepted Christ as his personal Saviour. The night that he was baptized, he said that he felt better than he had in a long time. He really looked like he was enjoying life. He was attending church and appeared to be enjoying it. I don't know what, but something went wrong. I am willing to trust him into the hands of the Lord, who knows all the answers.

Many times someone gives verbal or nonverbal clues and nobody really hears. I know of several suicides that could have possibly been prevented, if significant people in the person's life had heard the cry for help. If a relative or friend talks of suicide, or acts in a strange manner suggesting a struggle with suicide, recognize the signs, and believe there is danger. Someone may ask, "When I think there is danger of self-harm, what can I do?"

ASSESS THE DEGREE OF DANGER

The peace and calm of the mountain campground was broken by the screams of some boys who had been on a short hike. Their cries for help brought all the people out of their campers. One boy reached the campgrounds before the others, screaming: "A big black bear has Jim up a tree; he is going to eat him. Hurry, help him." Men got guns and rushed to rescue Jim from the bear.

When they reached the endangered boy, they were surprised to find him up a tree with a small black poodle at the base of the tree barking at him. "Why did you say it was a bear?" they asked the boy who came for help. He replied: "I wanted to prepare you for the danger. By thinking that it was a bear, you were not as afraid when you saw it was only a dog."

Though the illustration may not be believable, most of us find it hard to measure danger; we either minimize or maximize it. We usually swing to one of two extremes: a poodle becomes a bear or a bear becomes a poodle. When danger is involved, we often make a faulty interpretation of reality.

You cannot measure danger with a rule or yardstick, nor can you put it in a measuring cup. Yet, you may prevent a person from killing himself by estimating the amount of suicidal danger. Therefore, we ought to be sensitive enough to troubled people to estimate the seriousness of a suicide crisis. If involved with a person in a suicide crisis, you should first try to determine how great the danger is of the person harming himself.

EVALUATE THE SUICIDE PLAN

One day a mental hospital patient said that he was going to plant a garden. When asked where he would plant the garden, he said that he would plant it where his ward was now standing. When someone asked him where he would live when he tore down his ward for a garden, he said that he had already made plans for a place to live; he would move up to the second floor. Not a feasible plan, obviously.

When a person makes plans to end his life, his plans are usually realistic. Therefore it is important, when dealing with a suicidal person, to determine if the person has a plan for ending his life. If there is a definite plan, such as shooting himself with a gun, hanging himself with a rope, taking an overdose of drugs, jumping off a bridge, or some other deadly plan, the danger is much greater than when there is no definite plan. Also, if the person plans to shoot himself, does he own or have access to a gun? If he plans to hang himself with a rope, has he already acquired a rope? The degree of danger can also be determined by the method he plans to use for killing himself. For example, if the person has a handful of aspirins or a gun in sight, it is cause for alarm.

Experience with two people on the same day gave quite a contrast in the degree of danger. I saw a man with a definite plan for ending his life and a woman without a definite plan for killing herself. Even though the woman's family and the psychiatrist who referred her to me were very concerned that the woman would attempt suicide, she was not in any real danger of harming herself. An interview with her revealed that she had not given any thought to how she would commit the fatal act. Further sessions with her convinced me that she was not in any real danger of killing herself.

With the man it was much different. The family knew that he was very depressed but did not believe there was danger of suicide. Notwithstanding that suicide was not suspected, this man had already made plans for ending his life; he was an airplane pilot and planned to wreck his small plane.

Evaluation of his plan for killing himself convinced me that this man was in real danger. So I put in motion a treatment plan to keep him alive until we could move him out of his despair. First, I got his permission and convinced his family that his life was in danger. Next, I made a contract with him, which included among other agreements, that he would not fly his plane for an agreed period of time. He consented to being grounded until he could cope with his life. Then, he and I walked together to unravel his tangled life.

This man is now alive because he learned to manage his life; he realized that living his life was a better choice than death. Yet, if I had not taken his suicide plan seriously, he would have taken his last plane ride and wound have been grounded permanently. Determine the degree of danger by evaluating the person's plan for taking his life.

Somebody may ask. "Does a suicidal person always have a plan for killing himself, or do some people kill themselves on an impulse?" It is possible that some people kill themselves without any forethought, but I doubt it. I suspect that most people who commit suicide have planned their action. However, there is no guarantee that a person will not kill himself on an impulse. So, while suicide without forethought is possible, it is not probable. We can usually determine the degree of danger by evaluating the person's suicide plan, the type of plan, or lack of a plan. And, if a person has a definite plan for ending his life, we know that he is in danger of suicide.

SURVEY OF EMOTIONAL SUPPORT

Next in determining the degree of danger in a suicide crisis, try to find out whether the person is alone. Thoughts of suicide are much different when an individual is surrounded by people who are loving than when he is standing alone on a high bridge overlooking a river. If you should receive a call from someone contemplating suicide, determine where the person is. Is he alone? If he is, who is close by? Remember, the danger is very great for a person experiencing a suicide struggle while alone.

NOTATION OF PREVIOUS ATTEMPTS

Another procedure for the measurement of danger in a suicide struggle is investigation of previous suicidal attempts. A history of suicide attempts increases the danger. That a person has failed in attempts to end his life in the past is no guarantee that he will fail the next time, and failure in past experiences does not keep him from trying again. Rather, if he has tried before, he will be more likely to try again. Someone may say, "He didn't really try before; he just wanted attention; he is not going to kill himself." Another may say, "She has tried this act before; she will not actually kill herself; she does not really want to die." Wrong! Many people who kill themselves have previously tried to end their lives. If a person has tried before and is in a suicide crisis, he will likely try again, and probably succeed.

OBSERVATION OF DEPRESSION

A final question for you to pose when trying to find the degree of danger is twofold: Is the suicidal person depressed; is he coming out of a deep depression? A person is more likely to attempt suicide while coming out of a deep depression than he is when severely depressed. At any rate, try to check on symptoms of depression such as fitful sleep, loss of appetite, neglect of personal care, and withdrawal to a room. If the person is depressed, don't make the common mistake of urging him to "snap out of it." One does not just snap out of depression.

LEARN TO RECOGNIZE MENTAL ILLNESS

Mental health workers have made much progress in diagnoses of mental illness. Years ago, when people knew little about the cause and treatment of mental illness, crude methods were used for diagnosis. For example, one method was the water and spigot technique. A person believed to be mentally ill was placed before a pail of water under a dripping spigot; he was then given a spoon and assigned the task of dipping all the water out of the pail. If he tried to empty the pail with the water dripping, he was diagnosed as being insane. If he turned the spigot off and then dipped the water out of the pail, he was considered sane.

This method of diagnosis was, of course, ridiculous, as mental illness is not the same as mental retardation; many mentally ill people are very intelligent. Be that as it may, we need to be able to recognize symptoms of mental illness. Many books and pamphlets explain these symptoms.

You may prevent a person from killing himself, and others, by being alert to spot suicidal persons who are mentally ill. Every family needs to be alert to mental illness in any of the family members. And, every person who works with people in a church needs to be alert to recognize mental illness in any person in the church. When clues of suicide are noticed, symptoms of mental illness take on even more importance. When a mentally ill person is suicidal, there are at least three concerns that the family and acquaintances should have for the person: self-protection, protection for others, and understanding of any "religious" activity and talk.

PROTECT THE PERSON FROM SELF-HARM

As to self-protection, most people realize and accept that the family and society have a responsibility to protect a mentally ill person from harming himself. Nevertheless, there are many times when people who should detect danger fail to do so. It is ever so easy for mental health professionals to blunder at this point.

A patient once showed up at my office in a psychiatric hospital, frantic because the staff had decided to let her go home for a visit. I immediately realized that this was not the usual apprehensiveness seen in many mental patients before their first visit home. I soon learned why.

A voice kept telling this woman to kill herself. Another voice would then tell her not to kill herself. She felt more secure against harming herself while in the protected environment of the hospital, but was afraid she would obey the voice which told her to kill herself while away from the hospital. She would have likely killed herself if she had gone home at that time. If a mentally ill person, or any person for that matter, is suicidal, someone should give protection against self-harm.

PROTECT OTHERS FROM HARM

A big strong young man sat at a conference table with several staff members at the hospital. Before he was brought before the staff, his physician had presented his case history, which included much religious suicidal and homicidal thinking. Therefore, the conference had a three-fold purpose: We wanted to make a diagnosis, determine if the man was dangerous to himself or others, and project a treatment plan. The staff agreed on the diagnosis and treatment, but differed on whether the patient was dangerous; so the following interview was to determine whether others needed protection form this man:

AUTHOR: "Mr. Jackson, I understand that you are a religious man."

PATIENT: "Yes, sir, I am in direct contact with the Lord."

AUTHOR: "Do you want to tell us about you and the Lord?"

PATIENT: "I do nothing but what the Lord tells me to do. He says for me not to tell you about us."

AUTHOR: "You mean God is talking to you now?"

PATIENT: "He talks to me all the time."

AUTHOR: "Do you hear God talking with your heart, or hear him talking with your ears?"

PATIENT: "I hear His voice with my ears. God has a voice; He uses it to talk with me."

AUTHOR: "What would you do if God told you to kill the doctor sitting beside you?"

PATIENT: "I would not disobey God; I would kill the doctor."

Keep in mind that a mentally ill person who is suicidal may need close watching to prevent harm from coming to others. Often the harm will be directed toward significant people—members of the person's family, a friend, a fellow worker, or a lover. It is not uncommon to read or hear news of someone killing his or her mate in a murder-suicide. A suicidal, mentally ill person may randomly kill innocent bystanders and then take his or her own life.

It is a myth that all people who commit suicide are mentally ill, if psychotic is meant. But when a suicidal person is also homicidal, the killing is usually a senseless act by an irrational mentally ill person. If one is not mentally ill and plans to kill oneself, there is usually not any danger of the person harming others. Yet, even this statement has possible exceptions.

PROTECT FROM A "SICK RELIGION"

"Nancy has gone crazy over reading the Bible." These were the words of Nancy's friends and neighbors. They were sincere, intelligent people who loved Nancy and were concerned for her welfare. Nonetheless, they were sincerely wrong in their interpretation of her problem. Nancy did not become mentally ill because of reading the Bible; she started reading the Bible excessively when she realized that her world was falling apart. Reading the Bible will not make a person mentally ill; rather, it can make a person emotionally healthy. Reading the Bible did, however, become a problem for Nancy; it was distorted by her sick thinking. Consequently, during her illness she had a "sick religion."

Therefore, the third concern that people should have for the suicidal, mentally ill person, is an understanding of the person's religious talk and behavior. This is especially true of the family and church workers. Many times the ill person is crying out for help, but the cry is either ignored or misunderstood. For example, consider the severely depressed person who feels she has committed the unpardonable sin. Church workers often spend countless hours reading Scripture and counseling the sick person. Or, consider the mentally ill person who is constantly asking a pastor or Sunday School teacher about his or her salvation. Too often the church worker attempts to convince the person of some particular Scripture, when the sick person is seeking help because his world is crumbling around him.

The Bible is certainly important for any person, but the use of the Bible with certain mentally ill people is likely to make them more confused. When someone known to be mentally ill is discovered to be interpreting the Bible to his harm, then it is usually wise that he be prevented from reading the Bible. But it is not the Bible that is the cause of his illness; it is his illness that is the cause of his distorted interpretation of the Bible.

I am not suggesting that the Bible will make a person mentally ill. Is the Christian belief that God's love rescues one from the entanglements of sin conducive to mental illness? Christian experience gives one a new beginning, a fresh start, a clear slate: is that conducive to mental illness? Christian experience gives one forgiveness for his past, meaning for his present, and hope for his future. Will that cause mental illness?

Howbeit, it is imperative that the church worker or family member hear the person's cry for help, and assist the person in getting the help. if the church worker, or family member, can only understand that the sick person realizes that his life is falling apart, and he is reaching out for the most stable resource about which he has ever heard, this resource is, of course, God or the Bible.

However, if the person is experiencing defective or lost contact with reality, his thinking about God or the Bible will likely be "sick religion." But a person who becomes excessively interested in religion because of his illness—such as joining another church, reading his Bible all the time, or talking incessantly about religion—will probably forget about it when his condition improves.

I know of cases where a failure to recognize that the person was mentally ill, and consequently responding to the person as one would respond to a normal person seeking spiritual help, possibly caused the person to commit suicide. A mentally ill person who is suicidal, and suddenly becomes interested in the Bible, church, or some religious activity, does not need Scriptures quoted to him, placement in some church office, or baptism; he needs professional psychiatric help.

CONCLUSION

Even though suicide is a complex problem, if you want to help a person in the throes of suicide, you can do something to help. The general suggestions given in this chapter should give guidance; they provide a general approach to helping suicidal people. As you read the next chapter, you will become acquainted with some specific suggestions for helping people who are experiencing trouble with suicide.

6 HOW TO RESCUE A PERSON FROM SUICIDE—SPECIFIC SUGGESTIONS

Four beautiful caskets containing the bodies of an entire family, victims of a senseless killing, portray a tragedy. Bruce Litchfield, a 38-year-old supervisor for the Farmers Home Administration in Faulkton, South Dakota, killed his family and then killed himself. Someone described the husband and wife as people who had trouble making friends. But the saddest words are those spoken by the pastor of the church they attended. He was quoted as saying that the church just did not know how to reach them (*New York Times*, January 10, 1986).

Countless people, feeling alone and friendless, are hurting; but many good pastors and church members who really care do not know how to reach them. One man whose brother had killed himself said with a great amount of feeling: "If only I could have known how to help him!" Suicidal people appear to be beyond help, but this is in appearance only; they can be helped. Inability to aid them is usually the result of our limited understanding of suicide, rather than the complexity of the factors pushing the person toward self-destruction.

Throughout the land many people are beginning to realize that something can, and must be done about the suicide epidemic. At the University of California, Los Angeles, for example, each student's registration packet a year ago contained a six-page pamphlet alerting students to the danger signals of suicide.

Concern and prevention programs are also visible in many school districts. One such district is Glenbard High

School District 87 just west of Chicago. School personnel in this district have recognized that suicide is a serious problem, and have begun a program to do something about it. They realized that teachers are on the front line of recognition and referral; therefore they offer information and training for them.

Along with concerned efforts by mental health agencies and education institutions, some religious institutions are trying to battle the suicide epidemic. A healthy concern is especially visible in such efforts as the one put forth in the spring of 1985 by the Conference of Churches in Glastonbury, Connecticut. While clarifying their own interpretation of suicide, church people joined forces with other agencies and services to furnish information on suicide. They also engaged in efforts to prevent suicide.

Across the land people are asking: "How can I rescue a person from suicide?" Many people want information to help them understand this problem. They realize that efforts to decrease the suicide rate must be based on reliable suicide information.

Also, other factors enter into discussion of specific ways of suicide prevention: the degree of danger and age of the suicidal person. As to the age of the person who is in danger of harming himself, I will try to make the suggestions inclusive enough to include any age group. As to the degree of danger, there are at least three levels of danger: the incipient level, the crisis level, and the emergency level.

By incipient level I mean the beginning of the problem; the person is bothered by thoughts of harming himself; the problem has just become apparent to the suicidal person. By crisis level I mean the level of despair where the suicidal person is at a turning point; he will overcome his feelings or attempt to kill himself; his condition will become better or become worse. As to the emergency level, I mean that the person is beyond the crisis level; he is on the verge of attempting suicide. Let us consider these three levels of danger along with ways to help.

WHEN A PERSON THINKS OF SUICIDE

Nine frogs were sitting on a log. One frog took a notion to jump off. How many frogs were left on the log? This riddle, asked by small children to each other, is supposed to get the answer that eight frogs are left on the log. When all the children say eight frogs are left, the child then says: "You are wrong; one took a notion to jump off but then changed his mind and did not jump."

This little riddle, used by children to have fun, actually teaches an important human behavior principle. Having the thought did not mean that the frog was committed to jumping. He could go either way—stay on the log or jump from the log; so it is with a person who has a thought of harming himself.

How can one keep a suicidal person, still on the level of being bothered by thoughts of harming himself, from attempting suicide? Keep in mind that a person on this level of danger is not severely depressed. Also, he is not overcome with a feeling of hopelessness, uselessness, and helplessness. Neither has he attempted suicide in the past. Many people on this level make such remarks as: "Thoughts of killing myself sometimes come into my mind." "I wonder if life is worth living." The suggestions for this level of suicide danger are suggestions only; I recognize the impossibility of knowing for certain that the person has only occasional thoughts of self-harm.

■ *Suggestion No. 1: Get professional help.* Regardless of how insignificant the person's thoughts of suicide seem, one who has only occasional thoughts of killing himself needs a qualified counselor to aid him as he deals with his life struggle. This professional, whether a psychiatrist, psychologist, or a pastor, should be someone whose training and experience equips him for work with suicidal people.

How can one know the qualifications and experience, for example, of a psychiatrist or psychologist? Several sources for this kind of information are readily available: One may get helpful information from his mental health association; his pastor or physician may be able to guide him to the right person; several big cities have suicide prevention centers. Perhaps the most reliable source of information is an acquaintance who has experienced help for himself or a member of his family from a psychiatrist or psychologist, or even a pastor who has special training.

Someone may ask, "But how can I get a family member, a friend, or a co-worker to receive professional help?" First of all, don't try to trick a suicidal person. Usually an individual on this level of danger will go to someone for help. Suicidal thoughts are frightening; consequently, many people entertaining suicidal urges are eager to talk with someone. Sometimes the person will prefer to talk first with his pastor or physician.

■ *Suggestion No. 2: Seek to relieve pressures.* To rescue a person from his suicidal problem, try to relieve the pressures which trigger the suicide. The person having occasional thoughts of suicide may be under family pressure, work pressure, or financial pressure. While he or she is getting counseling, seek to identify any heavy burdens, needs, or problems pressuring the victim.

A child under pressure. If the person with the problem is a child, the family may be able to determine any pressure by talking among themselves. How well does the child fit into family life? Do family members have reasonable expectations of the child? Does the child have playmates? If he has, how does he get along with them? Are there pressures at school? Is there jealousy among the children? Does the family have financial problems? Does the child have reason to feel loved and wanted by the parents? Do the parents give firm, fair, and consistent discipline or structure to the child? How do the parents get along with each other?

When parents are able to ask such questions as these, and seek real answers, they can sometimes find the pressure which is bothering a troubled child. My experience counseling children reveals that almost all troubled children will tell what is troubling them, if they are asked in a pleasant manner.

A teenager under pressure. If the person with suicidal thoughts is a teenager, identification of his pressure will be more difficult. All teenagers experience developmental turmoil to some degree; they are neither children nor adults. Life during teen years is often rough—for some, rougher than it is for others. Teenagers want to do their own thing but most also want somebody to tell them what to do. Someone has called the teenage years a time of "whistling in the dark." Who can know the pressures of a severely troubled teenager? Still, identification of the pressures which bother a teenager may not be as hard as one thinks. At least three sources of information are available for concerned parents of teenagers.

1. Sometimes a teenager's peers will furnish information if they are also concerned about the suicidal person. However, a parent should be careful in this area of investigation; great damage may be done if the peers of one's son or daughter are questioned. Nevertheless, I have known times when a teenager confided to a friend that he had thoughts of killing himself; the friend then voluntarily told the troubled teenager's parents that he or she was worried about the son or daughter. However, if a parent prys into the affairs of a troubled teenager, he may push him into attempted suicide.

2. The school is a valuable source of information on teenagers. Teachers and guidance counselors often know more about teenagers than their parents know. Yet there are dangers in getting information from the school. I have known of cases where parents pried information out of school personnel and then unloaded it on their children. The ideal school-home relationship is one in which school people can communicate needs to parents without betraying confidences, and parents can communicate needs to school personnel without betraying confidences. Furthermore, if parents suspect that their son or daughter is having suicidal problems, they should seek a positive relationship of mutual trust with people at the school.

3. The best place for parents to get information about a teenager whom they suspect is struggling with suicidal thoughts is the teenager himself. Of course this source of information requires open communication lines between parents and children.

An adult under pressure. If the person with suicidal thoughts is an adult, the pressures on his life can be identified with less difficulty; however, the pressures may be much more difficult to relieve. When the person wanting to help a suicidal person is a member of his family, there are several areas for the family member to look for pressures.

First, the person wanting to help should look at family relationships. If the suicidal person is married, what kind of marriage does he have? If he has children, are they a blessing or a blight? What about the financial standing of the family? Is the person in debt with little money to pay his debts and take care of his family?

Second, the person wanting to help should get information about the suicidal person's work. Many people are under great pressure because of their working conditions; for many people work no longer gives any sense of personal achievement. Is the person who is having thoughts of suicide miserable in his work life? Has the person been denied a much deserved promotion? Has there been a change in management that has affected the individual—a sudden demotion, for example?

Third, the person wanting to help should find out about the suicidal person's church life. Church people are by no means exempt from discouragement or depression. For example, legalistic teaching may undermine a member's self-esteem. Under other conditions, church life itself may drain a person's energy because he is overworked. Even though most of us do too little church work, I have known people who were loaded down with responsibilities. I guess there is such a thing as church burnout; but most of the people whom I have observed with church burnout had burned out because of their feelings about their church work and/or a fellow worker rather than the work itself. Be that as it may, many people have mixed feelings toward their church work and religious activities.

■ *Suggestion No. 3: Enhance the person's self-esteem.* Martha, a bright three-year-old girl, was very conscious of her appearance; when she spotted mirrors at a carnival, she ran to one of them to look at herself. The next moment she frightened her parents with loud crying. They thought she had been hurt, and rushed to her. When they saw she was looking at herself in a trick mirror, their fear changed to laughter. Martha's reflection in the trick mirror alarmed her; she appeared to be as wide as she was tall. She did not like herself.

Many suicidal people see degrading pictures of themselves reflected back to them. Some pictures are accurate reflections of their personalities, and some are distorted. Whether these pictures are true or false, a person with low self-esteem doesn't like them. The person with suicidal thoughts will likely have a low opinion of himself. This is especially true of children and teenagers.

A child with low self-esteem. When the concern is with a child, there are many ways that parents and teachers can build up his confidence; they can find ways of making him feel good about himself. During his developmental years a child is forming a self-image; he is forming opinions about his own worth as a person; he needs positive feeling about himself to develop feelings of self-regard.

This is not to suggest that parents and teachers lie to a child. Children usually know when people are not sincere. Yet there are so many truthful comments people can make to children. Any teacher or parent can find something positive to say about a child.

A teenager with low self-esteem. Some teenagers are especially sensitive about their personal worth. During early teens when their bodies are developing, most teenagers go through a period of excessive concern about their appearance and feelings. Even during the middle and late teens, teenagers at times appear to regress to lower stages of development. A teenager who has suicidal thoughts likely has a low self-image. Parents are wise to major on the positive attributes of their children during their stormy teenage years. While giving to teenagers some stable outer structure, parents should also be sensitive to the developmental task of teenagers: development into young adults.

Eighteen-year-old Peggy was bothered by suicidal thoughts. Intelligent, energetic, and pretty, she, however, was afraid that she would eventually kill herself. Though Peggy had always tried to please her parents, she never quite succeeded. Because she had not received approval from significant people in her life, she had developed into an eighteen-year-old girl with a low self-esteem; she could not experience self-love. Notwithstanding the other conflicts in this girl's life, help for her had to include support from her parents. And, as is often true, the parents themselves had to have help before they could help their daughter.

An adult with low self-esteem. Adults who also have suicidal thoughts will likely have low self-esteem. If "normal" adults are helped by encouragement, how much more do adults with thoughts of suicide need encouragement? You can help an adult who has thoughts of harming himself by trying to build up the troubled person's opinions about himself. Many people go through life without having even a kind word spoken to them. If something or someone is constantly attacking the personal worth of a suicidal person while he is in counseling for his suicidal thoughts, that thing or person may have to be included in the counseling.

CRISIS LEVEL SUICIDE DANGER

The first days at an army base are rough for new recruits, Jasper was homesick, especially for Sally, his sweetheart. Really, his mind was on her rather than on his first days of training; thus he did not find it easy to follow the drill sergeant's orders.

Matters took a turn for the worse on the third day of training. His sergeant lined up all of the soldiers and gave a peculiar order. First, he said: "All married men take one step forward." Several soldiers stepped forward. Next, he commanded: "All single men take one step backward." The remaining soldiers stepped backward, that is, all except Jasper; he remained in his tracks.

The drill sergeant yelled: "Soldier, what does this mean? I said all married men forward, and you did not step forward. I said all single men backward, and you did not step backward. Soldier, explain your behavior!" Jasper, in a sheepish voice explained: "Sir, I am neither married nor single; I am courting Sally."

A person in a suicide crisis is somewhat like Jasper; in one sense he is neither dead nor alive; he is at a turning point: suicide or survival. A suicide crisis is a crucial time or state of affairs the outcome of which will make a decisive difference for life or death.

How then can any one of us rescue a person from a suicide crisis? An individual on this level of danger will not remain there very long. He will find inner resources to help him through the crisis; he will be helped by someone else; or he will act to kill himself. Here are suggestions for reaching out to someone in a suicide crisis.

■ *Act quickly; get professional help.* When an individual is evidently bent on suicide, pray as you rush to the telephone. Do not wait for a miracle. Delay can mean the difference between life and death. Tomorrow may be too late. Professional help is as near as your telephone. Reach out by phone, as AT&T urges.

■ *See that the person has protection from himself.* Keep

somebody with the suicidal person at all times. To leave a person in a suicide crisis alone in his room or house is to invite suicide. I have known of several cases involving people who would have been kept alive by the presence of another person.

■ *Remove any weapon or substance from the person's environment.* Even though a person who plans to commit suicide is usually capable of finding some way of killing himself, the removal of a gun or pills could prevent him from acting on an immediate impulse to take his life; the instant means of suicide is removed.

■ *Be cautious in efforts to help.* Be careful lest you do harm. A person in suicidal distress does not need criticism or put-down. He is on the bottom already. If he is already on the brink of suicide, such an approach by you could push him over. If you knock out any emotional props by weakening or removing his defense mechanism, you could cause him to kill himself. At this point in his life he does not need any "I-told-you-so" lectures. Any talk, attitude, or behavior that makes one feel less of a person, feel more of a failure, or feel hopeless or in the way may be harmful.

■ *Seek a way out of the crisis.* Try to offer some way of escape from the distress. Try to give the person some ray of hope to stabilize his life. Give him something to hold on to during the struggle. If you can identify the stress that triggered the crisis, you may be able to use it to help. For example, if the factor that triggered the episode is a loss of his job, you could possibly suggest some realistic hope of finding employment. If he has experienced disruption of a significant relationship, seek to assist him in mending the relationship, or encourage him into another positive relationship.

Keep in mind that the person needs some way out of the acute crisis. Some mental health workers have been successful with signed contracts, getting an agreement from the person that he will not kill himself for a certain period of time; this gives time for them to help him look for a way to ease the emotional pain.

■ *Show realistic optimism.* Be affirmative; act confident; communicate usefulness, helpfulness, and hopefulness. I myself have been successful at suggesting to a person in a crisis that someone needed him. Being needed gave him a reason to hold on to life. If one believes that someone really needs him, the belief could help him survive until the crisis is passed.

Also, I try to help a person in a crisis see that life can change; life can be different. If the troubled person sees some hope of improvement, he may be able to endure the emotional pain. The glimmer of hope gives strength to help the person through the crisis. When he can see the possibility of help for his intolerable condition, it becomes a positive force for remaining alive. Anyone who can help a person through the crisis will give a service of true Christian love. A superficial, veneer, or unrealistic attitude is not meant!

■ *Enlist emotional support.* If possible, enlist the support of the person's family and friends. The person in a suicide crisis feels alone in his struggle. He needs to feel that somebody understands and cares. You will need to exercise caution with this approach, though, because many suicidal people are crossed up with certain family members. Try to find somebody who cares and who wants to help.

■ *Seek other resources.* In many suicide cases you may consider tapping other resources to get help. The suicidal person may need the help of a law enforcement officer, the individual's physician, or a social worker. Even if you get the person through the crisis, he will still need additional help.

■ *Get the person into a hospital.* If indicated, and it usually is, the person in a suicide crisis needs to be admitted to a hospital; this will give to him continuous surveillance. Most people on this level of suicide danger need to be watched continuously. A hospital is able to give this care.

EMERGENCY LEVEL SUICIDE DANGER

Please keep in mind that the person on the emergency level of suicide danger has passed beyond suicidal crisis; he is moving toward suicide; he is ready to commit the suicidal act. A person on this level of suicidal danger already has the bottle of pills, holds a gun in his hand, or stands at a window ten stories from the ground. How then can you rescue a person on this level of danger? There simply are no easy answers. You are dealing with an emergency! Still you will want to do something.

The action you take in an emergency suicide case will be determined by many factors: Where you are in relationship to the suicidal person is important. The method the suicidal person is about to use for ending his life is also extremely significant. In view of all the possible circumstances involved, I will cite only two possible cases to make specific suggestions.

■ *A phone call emergency.* At 2 o'clock one morning you receive a phone call from a friend in a distant city. The friend says: "I have a gun in my hand and plan to blow my brains out. Life has lost all meaning for me. I have no reason to live; this is the end. I just called to tell you goodbye."

There are at least three things that you can do: (1) Keep the person on the line as long as possible; the suicidal person is not apt to pull the trigger of the gun as long as you are talking. (2) If someone else is with you, he can get to another phone and place a long-distance call to a crisis center, police, or a pastor. (3) You can use some of the suggestions listed under crisis level to try to talk the suicidal person out of suicide. For example, you have one strong factor—your mutual friendship—that you can use to try to prevent the suicide, pointing out that the suicidal person is very special to you and that you need him.

■ *A building-top emergency.* You may meet an emergency level of suicidal danger under different circumstances. Suppose that you are walking along the street one day and see a crowd looking up at a ten-story building. Suddenly you focus on a woman standing on a window ledge six floors up; someone says that the woman climbed out a few minutes ago and that her husband has been called at work. What possibly can you do to prevent her from jumping to her death? You realize that you know her from church and want desperately to help rescue her.

First, make certain that someone trained in dealing with emergencies is called to the scene. Many people, such as law enforcement officers, firemen, and rescue squad workers have some training for dealing with such emergencies, but they must be contacted instantly.

Second, try to talk to the woman on the building. People

without any special training in suicide prevention have talked suicidal people out of destroying themselves. If you can talk to the woman, you may be able to use some of the suggestions previously listed.

Believe that the woman in the suicide emergency wants to escape her miserable life, but does not necessarily want to be dead; she likely imagines that she will be rescued. Also, remember that the person has no hope of any improvement in her life; and she feels helpless in her hopeless condition. If you love people and want to help, you can use your understanding of the suicidal person's feelings and needs to convince the person in the suicide emergency that life can be different; there is hope for tomorrow!

SUMMARY

You can have a life-saving part in offering hope to hopeless people. Yet to do so, you must be willing to prepare yourself; and you must love enough to pay the price of preparation. The following steps will help prepare you for work with suicidal people:

1. Accept that we do have a problem with suicide.
2. Learn all you can learn about suicide.
3. Recognize suicide cries for help—signs and signals.
4. Identify resources for helping suicidal people.
5. Master suicide information that will help you work with suicidal people.
6. Become a person who relates to troubled people.
7. Believe there is hope for people in the throes of the suicide problem.
8. Act on what you are, know, and believe.
9. Live a life of faith and optimism.

7 A SUICIDE MISSION—HELP FOR HOPELESS PEOPLE

A caterpillar, an elongated wormlike creature which eventually becomes a butterfly or moth, survives by eating the leaves from trees. After a mother had spent some time explaining this little creature to her seven-year-old son and her five-year-old daughter, she saw them sitting, looking intently at a telephone pole. She walked out to where they were sitting and asked: "What are you doing?" The little boy responded: "We put a caterpillar on the pole and it is climbing up the pole; it thinks the pole is a tree. We want to see how disappointed it will be when it gets to the top and finds no food."

A church is God's tree of life where hungry souls should find food for spiritual, and sometimes physical, survival. In the truest sense, many are not able to survive with their bodies because their spirits are starved. Souls in despair are often surprised and disappointed when they fail to find survival food. They come to a church expecting help; they go away many times with empty minds and burdened hearts. They seek some way to deal with their despair and need spiritual nourishment for their souls. Churches have an opportunity, but more so a *responsibility*, for the suicide epidemic sweeping across the nation.

The suicide epidemic is real; it is not something we can ignore because we think it will go away. Almost everyone believes that suicides will increase in number as tensions mount. When faced with problems in the past, churches met the challenge with innovative programs and services; Christians led the way with whatever they needed for meeting the task. Years ago, when people recognized the problem of human illiteracy, Christians took the lead in the establishment of schools. Likewise, when people realized that sickness was a human challenge, Christians blazed the health trail by building hospitals to care for the sick. To reach out to the poor, Christians established Gospel rescue missions and gave hungry people both physical and spiritual food.

Christians are now confronted with another great human need—a suicide epidemic. If we are to meet and master this need with the same creative faith, we need to examine three questions: What can churches do for suicidal people? What can Christians do when they are confronted with someone in a suicide crisis? What can a person do when thoughts of suicide bother him? Let us consider these questions one by one.

WHAT CHURCHES CAN DO FOR SUICIDAL PEOPLE

Television commercials are often better than television programs. One such fascinating commercial was the one little dab of a certain hair tonic that turned a young man into an irresistible Romeo; just one little dab made all the girls chase him. The commercial meant to demonstrate that one little dab will do it. Many young men were likely disappointed. Imagine a young fellow putting one little dab on his hair and getting no response from the girls. No, one little dab probably won't do it.

Many churches should learn a similar lesson; one little dab will not give troubled people the help they need. Churches must take seriously the suicide epidemic, and meet the needs of these troublesome times. But what, really, can churches do to curb the spread of this epidemic?

Along with a ministry of teaching and preaching, churches ought to minister directly to troubled people. This ministry should, of course, include help for people who are struggling with suicide. Even though churches have done very little for these people in the past, most actually care about all people and want to help; failure to help in the past, however, has not been due to a lack of love and concern but to a lack of understanding of suicide.

Now that information is available for training church members for helping suicidal people, many churches are beginning programs to help people in despair. Someone may say, "Other than publish spiritual truths, what can my church do to help?" This is an important question, because knowledge about the suicide problem and concern for suicidal people, alone, will not solve the problem. Churches must have programs to get church members involved in specific intervention services. Any church, regardless of its size, can begin a program for the prevention and treatment of suicide. Hope for the hopeless is revealed in Christian service. Let's now examine a projected suicide program which offers hope for these hopeless people.

■ *Step No. 1: Develop an informed membership.* The ship was damaged and rapidly taking on water; soon it would sink. The passengers on the ship were from several countries, some underdeveloped and backward countries. Because they spoke different languages, many could not communicate with each other. Since many had never been on a ship before this voyage, they did not even know what a life jacket was. To make matters worse, the passengers had not received any instructions for emergencies. So the emergency had thrown the crew and passengers into a state of turmoil and confusion.

However, people who did know about life jackets were getting them and jumping into the ocean. One confused fellow watched as one passenger after another picked up a life jacket and jumped. Finally, he thought he had figured out what was happening, so he picked up a nearby heavy object and jumped into the ocean!

A church should begin its suicide program with an orientation workshop to inform the members of the church about suicide. The average church member is either uninformed or misinformed about this epidemic. Thus an orientation workshop could refute suicide myths while teaching some basic suicide facts. While leading church workshops on suicide, I have observed much interest in the subject. Participation in the discussion periods has been amazing; people want information on suicide. Many are realizing that this problem may touch their lives. An orientation workshop, alone, will help many people. It will let church members know there is hope for the hopeless.

■ *Step No. 2: Work toward a redeeming fellowship.* While a group of inner-city sixth-graders were deep in a forest on a science field trip, they got more learning than they expected. Walking through the woods, they came upon a crab apple tree. They had never seen a crab apple tree, and wanted to explore its fruit. They had, though, eaten pickled crab apples and saw that this fruit was different only in color from them. Yes, you are right; they rushed to the tree and each youngster plucked a crab apple.

Imagine the change that took place in this class of children when they bit into the sour apples. According to the teacher, she had a "crabby class"; the laughter and talk turned sour. The members of this sixth-grade class will always remember their crab apple experience for two reasons: the sour experience and the new class name. Class members were nicknamed "crab apple cadets."

When one views the sour outlook of some church members, he wonders if their churches have had a similar experience; the nickname *crab apple cadets* gives a vivid description of them. Rather than a spirit of hope, the spirit of many churches has turned sour, reflecting a morbid picture of gloom. To be a redeeming fellowship, a church must offer hope for hopeless people.

A church should be a redeeming fellowship to counteract the feeling of hopelessness that permeates our society. Christian fellowship is a fellowship of hope; thus it radiates hope, even beyond the fellowship of a church. Also, this hope touches every aspect of our lives. Consequently, we are aware of our frailty but not defeated by it; we are aware of our apartness but not overcome with loneliness; we are aware of the pressures of life but not overwhelmed by them; we are aware of human tragedy but not depressed by it.

This redeeming fellowship of hope gives us acceptance, understanding, support, and direction. The redeeming fellowship is a spiritual resource for God's people. It is a refuge from the storms of life; it is a place of reinforcement for the struggles of life; it is a place of renewal for the failures of life; it is a place of hope for the hopelessness of life.

Much of our feeling of aloneness, our feeling of hopelessness, and our feeling of helplessness could be changed by participation in the redeeming fellowship of a local church where Christ is honored. Man finds himself by losing himself, and loses the pain of self-awareness by fellowship with God and others; therefore, a church has a wonderful opportunity but an awesome responsibility. It can be a haven of rest for the weary and the lonely.

In the church people can lean much on the relationship of love that penetrates the aloneness of humanity. One can experience a continuous opening of his inner self to the presence of God and the presence of others. When one can "practice the presence of God" and accept the love and warmth of the Christian fellowship, he can live in the aloneness of his inherited apartness without excessive pain.

If there is any place on earth where a person feels loved, wanted, and a part of the life of others, it should be in the fellowship of a church. When one enters a church he should feel that others accept and love him. When he leaves a church, he should leave with the awareness that church people really care about him. He knows that they will give to him emotional support; he feels that these people understand him; he believes that he can depend on them. Church fellowship could be a significant force against the hopelessness of the suicide epidemic.

■ *Step No. 3: Establish an identification and referral service.* I once heard a speaker tell of a goat that lost its identity. Its owner was shipping it on the train to a friend in a distant city, when it became a real problem for the porter and conductor. As goats are rather strange creatures, it had been nothing but trouble since they loaded it on the train. The troublesome goat finally exhausted the patience of the porter; he discovered that the ticket they had put on it was gone; it had eaten the ticket. Rushing up to the conductor, he said: "I have had it with that goat; he done ate up where he is going."

Many people have destroyed where they are going; they are identified only by despair and suicide. Identity as creatures of God is essential for their survival. Churches must recognize that they are important; God loves them.

Churches large and small could have an identification and referral service for troubled people, including suicidal people. Such a service could meet two special needs in the battle against suicide. In the first place, people with suicidal tendencies could be identified. In the second place, when identified they could be referred to a resource for therapy.

Far too often a member of a family struggles alone with suicide because no other member of the family recognizes the danger. Then also many times a family recognizes that a family member is in trouble but for some reason they fail to get help for him. Often people are embarrassed when they go for help, not knowing where to go or what to do.

Church members also often fail to identify a suicidal problem, or fail to get help for an individual when they do identify it. When a church knows about someone who needs help, the person's family should be contacted. When church members have the opportunity of giving emotional support and directional guidance to a family, they should do so in love. When a suicidal person does not have a family, or has an irresponsible family, church members themselves may have to give emotional support and assistance to the person.

■ *Step No. 4: Create a crisis line.* Our generation has made much progress in the communication field; for example, consider our telephones. Modern telephones with modems and answering machines are much better than the old crank phones and even more recent phones that required that you give an operator your number. Use of a telephone was not so easy during those days. In fact there were many mix-ups in communication with older telephones.

We have made much improvement in telephone communication; almost every home has a phone. The average American citizen lets his fingers do his walking; yet phones could be put to much better use, especially for emergencies. Churches could use them for helping troubled people.

Many counties and cities have crisis lines, which are served by volunteer workers, trained to assist people in crises. Inasmuch as this help is available to any person in distress, a person in a suicide crisis may use these lines to call for help. These volunteer workers make a wonderful contribution; however, many people in suicide crises do not know about these volunteer workers, or fail to call them when they do know about them. This is not a negative reflection on crises line workers; while helping train volunteer workers, I observed their dedication and service to crises line work; volunteer workers for a crisis line do a wonderful work.

Howbeit, often there is a gap between a person in a suicide crisis and contact with the crises line workers. Churches could fill that gap. Already in some churches either a secretary or the pastor acts as a crises line worker. In other churches people experience difficulty in reaching someone, even in cases of emergency. Every church could have a crisis line with trained people taking the calls. If a church would enlist and train only a few of its members for crises work, much help could be given to troubled people, including suicidal people. These workers could at least guide people to help.

■ *Step No. 5: Organize an interaction group.* Every church ought to have an interaction group, as described: such a resource would be of great value to members and nonmembers. Even though group interaction would be helpful for most any person, participation in such a group would be especially helpful to a person in despair. Involvement with an interaction group could benefit a suicidal person as follows:

■ *Participation in an interaction group would help move a lonely person out of his aloneness.* The person would feel that he was a part of the group; he would gain a sense of belonging. Many suicidal people make such remarks as: "I feel so alone in the world."/"I feel cut off from everybody."/"There seems to be a wall between me and other people." Other suicidal people do not talk about their feelings of aloneness but withdraw from contact with other people; they live alone in their rooms much of the time. Some suicidal people continue to live in the physical presence of other people, yet they remain aloof from others; they cut off interaction and communication from their families and friends.

Regardless of the lifestyle of a person who feels alone, the emotional pain is real; he needs freedom from his isolation. When a person signals by verbal or nonverbal behavior that he is a prisoner of aloneness, he needs human contact. Participation in a church interaction group would give human contact and emotional support.

■ *Participation in an interaction group could help a suicidal person in dealing with his inner storm.* Such involvement offers a safety valve to people who tend to be overcome by their emotional turmoil. It gives opportunity for a mind-cleaning to ventilate feelings that produce suicidal thoughts. The suicidal person could talk about the feelings deep inside that submerge him in despair. He could feel comfortable for the unbottling of his real thoughts. Talk of what he really felt and thought may bring some relief from his emotional pain.

When the person afflicted with depression can empty the poison from his mind and unscrew the mental lid from pent-up emotions, he experiences relief. Such is certainly included in the biblical admonitions, "Bear ye one another's burdens," and "Confess your faults one to another."

■ *Participation in an interaction group could help a suicidal person deal with his outer storm.* A person in despair must have help for the pressures which triggered his despair. The unbearable pressure may have come from his family, his work, or even his church. Regardless of the source of one's problems, interaction with other people could increase his problem-solving ability. When one views his problems from the pit of suicidal desperation, he sees no way of solving them. Group interaction could help move him out of the despair to give him a new view of his problems. Along with the new view of his problems, the suicidal person could gain a better understanding of his outer world. The group interaction would enable him to solve his problems rather than be overcome by them.

■ *Participation in a church interaction group could move a suicidal person to a meaningful use of Bible study and prayer.* For example, the group could interact by studying Bible promises or learning to pray, leading to a genuine relationship with the Lord rather than an external form of activity without meaning.

First, consider how a church interaction group could use Bible study to help people, especially suicidal people. Many people, bothered by suicidal thoughts, know about the Bible. Most suicidal people likely have been exposed to the Bible in some way. They have heard it taught in a Sunday School class; they have heard it preached in church worship services; some of them have read it. Yet for some reason the Bible has not spoken to their need. How could a church interaction group make a difference?

1. A church interaction group could make a difference in a person's study of the Bible by making the message of the Bible personal. Too often, even active Christians tend to generalize the Bible message. As members of an interaction group interact with each other and a trained group leader, they could be trained to interact with Bible truth. This could occur in two ways. When a member of the group shares a personal problem or need, the group supports the member as he examines his problem or need; the group then interacts in a search of the Bible to find a passage which will give a personal message to the person who has shared his problem or need.

2. Next, a church interaction group could make a difference in a person's study of the Bible by training him how to let the Bible speak its message to him. When we consider our tendency to speak to the Bible rather than letting the Bible speak to us, we realize how great the problem must be for a suicidal person—a person overcome by inner turmoil and outer pressure. If we who are normal tend to bring meaning to the Bible rather than let the Bible have meaning for us, the tendency must be greater for people who are submerged in suicidal thinking.

Mixed-up people do not hear the message or distort the meaning of the Bible because their confused thinking colors their interpretation. A trained group leader could aid people in hearing the message of the Bible. Role playing of Bible study is helpful in this type of training.

3. Finally, a church interaction group could make a difference in a person's Bible study by training him to search the Bible for passages which relate to his specific feelings and needs. A person with thoughts of suicide usually has inadequate or broken relationships with significant people in his life; there are Scriptures which guide one in establishing positive relationships with significant others. Ghosts from the past may haunt a suicidal person; the Bible gives God's recipe for solving the problems and sins of the past. The future is dark and dismal for a person who thinks of killing himself; the Bible radiates hope.

Second, meaningful prayer could also be important for a person who is bothered by thoughts of self-harm. I am not suggesting that a suicidal person become involved in some prayer system—a pattern for prayer. A person struggling with a suicide problem needs a relationship, not a system. How then could an interaction group with a trained leader help a person in the throes of suicide become involved in prayer?

A church interaction group could give group members training in prayer. From their prayer life they could actually experience several truths about prayer. The members of the group could discuss such truths as these: One may confess his true feelings when praying, because God already knows how the person feels (Matt. 9:4); an unworthy feeling, when confessed, brings God's blessings (Luke 18:13-14); when a Christian is weak—helpless—the strength of the Lord is manifested in his life (2 Cor. 12:7-10); faith is essential for successful praying (Matt. 21:22).

The interaction group could then become a prayer group, with each member experiencing meaningful prayer. If Christians who are bothered with thoughts of suicide learn the secret of meaningful prayer, their prayer life will make a difference; it will strengthen their lives.

Why should some people think it strange when Bible study and prayer reinforce one's life? True religion is the most healing and transforming force on earth.

The value of prayer and Bible study as a resource for Christian living is not fully understood and used. At a time when many of my colleagues are modifying behavior by behavior modification principles and procedures, Christians have access to the most powerful life-changing principles there are on earth—prayer and Bible study. I hasten to add, however, that even though these life-changing principles are on earth, they tie in to unearthly power, the power of the Lord of earth and heaven.

HOW CAN A CHRISTIAN HELP A SUICIDAL PERSON?

"Bear ye one another's burdens, and so fulfill the law of Christ" (Gal. 6:2). This verse teaches that a person is not to live his life in neutral. If one is stuck in neutral, he will not help with the burdens of troubled people. When I am tempted to be a passive participant of life, I remember an automobile which I once owned.

In most ways this automobile was a wonderful vehicle. Its appearance was beautiful; it shined like a silver star. Its brakes were effective, giving me a secure feeling. Its horn made a delightful sound; it sounded like a hoarse cow. The power under the hood was the envy of other young men; the motor purred like a Persian kitten. This automobile was an excellent vehicle; that is, with one exception—it became stuck in neutral.

I learned a lesson from that automobile, which every person ought to learn: one goes no place when stuck in neutral. A Christian who so lives will not bear the burdens of troubled people.

A group can give service which an individual cannot render by himself. Nevertheless, there are many times when a Christian stands alone to give individual service; he meets a need which nobody else can meet; he stands by himself to help someone in distress. So it is with suicide: any Christian may be confronted by someone in a suicide crisis. The confrontation may take place in his own home by a member of his family. Someone at his place of work may cry out to him for help. A member of his church may give a warning of his intention to kill himself. A relative or friend may call a church member on the phone and confide to him suicidal intentions. When the cry for help is to a Christian, a member of a local body of believers, he stands alone with a burden for responsible action.

One who works with suicidal people is often asked, "What can I do if a person tells me that he plans to kill himself?" Even though there are not any "cut-and-dried answers" to this question, most any church member can do something constructive in such a situation. Let us discuss two hypothetical cases. Consider the suggestions given in the following situations.

THE CASE OF THE LONELY CHURCH MEMBER

While standing in front of his church talking casually with another church member, James, a dedicated Christian, is taken completely by surprise. Without warning, the man confides to James that he is thinking about killing himself. Though James loves the Lord and faithfully attends his church, he has never prayed in public, never taught a Sunday School class, or engaged in any other such leadership role.

So James is dumbfounded when the other member of the church tells him: "I don't fit in with people. I exist in a world of my own. I'd rather be dead than have this terrible feeling of loneliness. You don't know the pain of being all alone in this world. Since my wife died, things have gone bad for me. On top of all this, my business is in trouble. Really, I have nothing to live for anyway. I came to church this morning hoping to get these terrible thoughts out of my mind. Just yesterday I loaded my pistol to kill myself but could not do it." Remember, James, who is hearing this, is not a psychologist or psychiatrist who knows how to handle a suicide problem. He is not even a leader in his church. What can he do to help this man?

First, James can listen to this man's cry for help. Yet, to do so, he must be silent long enough to hear this man's expression of mental and emotional pain. When someone expresses mental and emotional pain to us, we tend to stifle his expression of hurt. We want to shut off the expression of hurt because of our own insecurity, not because of feelings for the hurting person. We feel threatened by the expression of frightening thoughts or intentions. Being moved by our insecurity, we try to change the subject, or try to convince the person that he is not serious. Many times we slam the mental and emotional door in the face of a person crying out for help. Hopefully, James will control this human tendency and listen to the man.

Far too often we shut out the human cry for help. James does not have to be a professional counselor, or even a church leader, to listen to the other church member. Neither do you. Any person can button his lips and listen to another person in distress.

Second, James can tell the other church member that he loves him and wants to help him. Notwithstanding the other variables in this case, one thing is certain. This man is reaching out for someone who cares. His trust and confidence in James is demonstrated by the way he confides in him. Consequently, James may be able to communicate to the suicidal man that he is not alone, that he is willing to be his friend. Inasmuch as the man trusted James enough to tell him about his suicidal intentions, he will likely trust James when he says that he will walk with him in resolving his problem.

It is important that a suicidal person trust the person trying to help him. He must believe that the person is trustworthy and sincere. If the would-be helper says that he loves him, the suicidal person will want to be certain that he speaks sincere words of love. Sometimes a person in trouble will test a would-be helper to determine his sincerity and trustworthiness. Suicidal people who feel unworthy and helpless are quick to sense a lack of sincerity or superficial love.

Take as example Ellen, a twenty-five-year-old wife and mother, who became depressed and called for an appointment with her pastor. After three sessions with him, she felt comfortable enough in the counseling relationship to tell him about her suicidal thoughts. Prior to her fourth scheduled appointment, Ellen considered how she would tell him about her frightening thoughts. An hour before the 2 o'clock appointment, the church secretary called to tell Ellen that the pastor had an emergency and would have to see her the next week.

Even though she had "psyched" herself up to tell the pastor about her fear of harming herself, and was disappointed that she would not see him for another week, Ellen realized that pastors do have emergencies and must adjust their schedules.

However, when the church secretary called the next week to change the appointment once again, Ellen became extremely depressed. Soon her husband came home from work and told her that the pastor's emergency the week before was a meeting with a representative of a fundraising organization. Ellen felt that her pastor surely loved money more than he loved her; she felt rejected by the one person in the world from whom she expected help. By this time she was more depressed than ever; consequently, the feeling of rejection triggered her attempted suicide.

Many pastors, as well as most of us, do have busy schedules. It is difficult to keep priorities in the right order. But all of us need to be sensitive to people. After three sessions with Ellen, surely the pastor would have realized that Ellen needed his help desperately. Ellen's case undoubtedly reminded the pastor that he had not been sensitive enough to Ellen's need. The last thing she needed was to be rejected by someone she had trusted.

If, as is apparent sometimes, suicide is hostility turned in on one's self, love is the answer for some people who struggle with suicide. We are commanded to love our neighbor, but some of us find it impossible, because we do not have the proper love for ourselves. However, when God reveals Himself to the core of one's being, and there is a positive response, a new relationship is begun. One accepts God and is accepted by God. Because one is loved, he can love others; because he is accepted by God and himself, he can accept others. Certainly, Christians are supposed to be known by love. The new relationship with God, self, and others is to find expression in worship and fellowship with God, and also fellowship with other Christians, and love for all people.

Suicidal people who feel unworthy and helpless usually respond to sincere love. If they can realize that God loves them in spite of their miserable feeling, and if they are convinced that other people really love them, they may be able to open their lives to help. When a suicidal person is able to open his life to love, some of his hostility will be changed to love. His hate of life, which has now been turned inward to become hate for himself, may lose some of its strength. The transforming power of love is wonderful.

I learned the power of love one Saturday afternoon early in my Christian life. A man who lived down the road from us, delighted in criticizing me to other people. Even though he professed to be a Christian and was a leader in our church, he tried to kill my influence in the church.

On this hot Saturday afternoon, as I was on my way home, I saw a fire just ahead of me. When I arrived at the fire, I saw the man in a wooded area near his home fighting the fire by himself. Alone, there was no way he could stop the fire; two people could probably bring the fire under control.

Suddenly I realized that this situation presented one of the biggest challenges of my life. It was really a tough decision; should I stop and help him or continue down the road? Immediately I thought of what seemed to be three good reasons why I should not help him. It was hot; why should I fight fire in 100-degree heat? Next, the man obviously despised me. In the third place, I was wearing new white trousers. I looked at my trousers and then looked at the man, alone, fighting fire.

It would have been so easy to keep going; that is, if love had not entered the picture. But love overcame all my logic, including my new white trousers. And because love won, I won. Not even the ruined pants could dim the personal victory of loving the unlovely. If I had relied on my own strength, the new trousers would have won the debate. However, with the love of Christ, I was able to move out of my aloneness to share myself and enter the aloneness of another person, even a person who had not shown love toward me. My human frailty was transformed by love.

Love decisions are not always easy. Many times we behave like the little woman who had so much trouble with her husband. When she talked with her pastor about her "no good" husband, he asked if she had tried "heaping coals of fire upon his head," referring, of course, to the admonition in the Bible (Rom. 12:20). The little woman replied, "I have not tried coals of fire, but I threw some hot dishwater on him, and that didn't do any good!"

Rather than turn hostility outward or inward, we can experience the grace of God to turn hate to love. This is the opposite of trying to deny or cover up our hostilities. When hostility is bottled up inside of us, it eats away at our mental and emotional life like a cancer. On the other hand, when hostility is confessed, forgiven, and cleansed, it is replaced by love. Hostility destroys either other lives or our own lives; love enhances and extends life.

This is not to imply that love is a substitute for therapy with a person trained to help suicidal people. A person so trained can give the kind of treatment a suicidal person needs. He will be able to determine the degree of suicidal danger; he will be able to determine whether the person is mentally ill; he will be able to determine the amount of depression that the person is experiencing; he will help the person understand and resolve his suicidal thoughts and feelings; he will help the person relate to his environment in a more constructive manner; he will, if indicated, get the person into a hospital where he will be protected from self-harm.

When therapy is indicated for a suicidal person, and it usually is, love can lead the way toward getting professional help. When one expresses suicidal thoughts, love him enough to get help for him.

■ *Third, James can encourage his fellow church member to get help for his problem.* Assurance that he will go with the man to the pastor will offer a beginning place for his Christian brother to get help. James must realize that without professional help this man will likely kill himself. If he can get the man to the pastor, hopefully the pastor will know the route to someone trained in suicide prevention and treatment.

■ *Fourth, regardless of the help given by professionals, this suicidal man needs a reason for living.* He needs to escape his feeling of aloneness. He needs help for his feeling of helplessness. Evidently he was very close to his deceased wife. Since her death, he has not developed any new significant relationships. James can help him overcome his feeling of aloneness by getting him involved with other people. He can arrange for the man to be included in activity and conversation; church life offers many opportunities for such involvement. Sunday School classes, choirs, recreational activities, and worship services are only a few of the activities which provide opportunity for involvement with other people.

Perhaps, though, a word of caution is needed at this point. One's presence at an event or activity does not necessarily mean involvement with the event or activity. Church leaders—and the Jameses of the church—should make certain that no one is left out of conversation and activity. When some people suffering the intense pain of aloneness attend religious or social events, they feel like outsiders. This feeling may intensify their problems. While such people should not be pressured or embarrassed, we—the Jameses—need to include them in conversation and activity.

For example, in small group conversation direct the talk to a person who may feel excluded from the group. The following sentence illustrates this communication principle: "John, you are familiar with that city." If John says nothing but yes, he has a clue that he is a part of the conversation.

While positive human relationships are not a substitute for therapy, success in treatment is much related to human relationships. James should get his suicidal friend involved with other people. His loneliness is not caused by a loner personality, but rather by the loss of his wife. When a husband and wife live for years in a marriage relationship, depending on each other for emotional support, death of one spouse often leaves the other one in excessive loneliness.

Whether this man's business problems are symptomatic of his distraught life, or an unwelcome visitor to add to his distraught life, matters little in the outcome. He now feels lonely and helpless.

■ *Fifth, James can witness to his Christian faith.* To bare his soul to another in the first place, this troubled man must have seen something special in his fellow church member. Perhaps he had observed James and knew that he loved people; he must have believed that he could trust this member of his church. I am not suggesting that James preach to him, or try to shame him. This poor man does not need any put-down; he is already on the bottom. I am suggesting that he share his own experience of living for the Lord. But what he says must be real in his own life.

James will not do this sharing in a proud or boastful manner. He will share with the other man in the same spirit which the other man has shared with him. He will admit that he too is only a human, a human with problems. But along with the admission of his own human frailty, his own hardships, his own need for help, he will witness to the source of strength for his survival. He may express his witness with words such as:

"Life is sometimes rough. I know I would miss my wife if she died. I am thankful, though, for the presence of the Lord. Every day of my life I need His help more and more.

"From a human viewpoint I don't see my way through the hardships of life. I then realize that the Lord has promised to be with me in my troubles; He has promised to see me through my tribulations. There have been times when life seemed hopeless; then my life changed. The Lord loves us regardless of our feelings. Life can change. Life can be different."

■ *Sixth, James can try to convince this suicidal man that he is needed.* There are at least three possible approaches he could make in communicating this message to the man: (1) James could get the man to assist him in some good deed for a sick person or somebody else who needed help. (2) He could get the pastor of the church to enlist the man in some service in the church. (3) He could ask the man to do him a personal favor of some kind. If the man knows that somebody needs him, he will have a reason for living.

As I was writing this book, a severely depressed man came for his first therapy session. This disturbed man, an important government official, was struggling with suicide. When asked if he had considered how he would kill himself, he gave specific plans for taking his life. During the session I guided his conversation to a discussion of people who needed him. By the end of the session he had begun to gain some control over his despair. This improvement was only one step, a very short step, out of his despair. It did, though, give to him some emotional support during the suicide crisis.

THE CASE OF A TUNED-OUT TEENAGER

The other case involves a suicidal teenager, Bryan. Early one morning Pastor Jones received a telephone call from a frantic mother. She was afraid that her fourteen-year-old son would do something drastic. Recently he had been acting strangely. Bryan stayed in his room most of the time, coming out only to eat. His only response when spoken to was, "Stay off my case." A week ago he refused to attend school.

After explaining to the pastor that she knew her son was not on drugs, the mother started crying and told him what had just happened. Realizing that something must be done, she had gone to Bryan's room and confronted him about his strange behavior. The words he blurted out stunned and frightened her: "Nobody loves me. I can never please anybody. Janet [his sister] is Miss Perfect. Daddy criticizes me all the time. Now, even Betty, [his girlfriend] hates me. I wish that I could disappear. Everybody will be sorry when I am dead." The mother believed that her son's life was in danger. She began pleading: "Help us, Pastor! What can we do?"

Pastor Jones must make a decision which could result in either life or death. What can he do? He could shift into a pious voice and tell the mother that he will pray for them. He could suggest that the father take control and "straighten the young man out." He could suggest that the mother read the biblical passage to Bryan that says that children should honor their fathers and mothers. He could tell the mother to give him a few days to cool off; if he still felt upset, he would be happy to have a talk with him.

Don't laugh. Similar advice is given to people, but an alert pastor will not respond in such a foolish manner. He will realize that this mother's fears are realistic and try to help her. How can he help? Acting wisely, Pastor Jones will take steps as follows:

■ *Step No. 1.* He will encourage the mother to protect her son from himself. He will ask her to make this protection as inconspicuous as possible. She can find some reason for somebody to be close by him at all times. The pastor suspects that Bryan has broken up with his sweetheart; he knows that breakups may trigger suicide in certain teenagers.

■ *Step No. 2.* Pastor Jones will try to develop a positive relationship with this boy and encourage the family to do the same. However, one who assumes such a role with a person who feels alone must be willing to endure a cool reception, or possibly some insults. Often absorbed in his self-pity, the suicidal person may signal that he does not want to be bothered. Many times a person suffering the pain of aloneness pushes from him the thing he wants the most—another person. On the contrary, many suicidal people are eager for a relationship; they are receptive to overtures of friendship or love.

It is not unusual for members of a family to withdraw from one member of the family because they believe he wants to be left alone. Pastor Jones will want to remind them that a family member who feels isolated needs the love and support of his family. This is especially true of teenagers, he will point out. While a teenager's privacy should be respected, a family should not permit a teenager to withdraw into an emotional shell of aloneness. A wise family keeps the communication lines open to all the family members. When one person hears another person give a signal of aloneness, he can help by "going the extra mile" to build a positive relationship.

■ *Step No. 3.* Pastor Jones will assist in getting Bryan to a psychologist or psychiatrist trained in working with suicidal people.

■ *Step No. 4.* The pastor will give emotional support to this family but will encourage them also to get professional counseling. He realizes there may be unhealthy family processes: namely, unrealistic parental expectations and sibling rivalry. Whatever the family problems in the past, the family now has new problems to solve. A teenager's place in the family is significant in his personal functioning; help for the family will also be help for the son.

Pastor Jones will also need to be cautious in giving support to this family. In a family crisis the members of a family tend to blame each other for the presenting problem—the symptom of family stress. The pastor will want to guide the family away from assignment of blame to help for the problem. For after all, it is not a matter of blaming the culprits, but a matter of healing the victims.

■ *Step No. 5.* This helpful pastor will explore the possibility of using another teenager as a healing agent for the suicidal boy. Many times a young person will respond more quickly to one of his peers. Of course, there are many factors to be considered in this case. One, in particular, is the boy's therapist; the pastor will need some consultation with the psychologist or psychiatrist. If the therapist and the boy's family agree with the idea, the pastor will get a Christian young person, who relates well to other young people, to take some time with the distressed boy.

When a well-adjusted teenager shows friendship with a teenager who feels left out, there is spontaneous attention given to the teenager by his other peers. Success in using this approach is dependent upon the character of the teenager who tries to help. He must help because he cares about others; also, he must keep the arrangement in confidence. As the influence of teenagers upon each other is compelling, peer relationship is a positive force in teenage suicide work.

CONCLUSION

In this chapter we have considered the great opportunity for Christian service; we have examined what a church and individual members of a church can do for suicidal people. In the next chapter we will consider what a suicidal person can do for himself.

8 ACTIONS TO TAKE WHEN BOTHERED BY THOUGHTS OF SUICIDE

Joy was a joyful Christian. Throughout the region she had put a sparkle in people's lives. Even her nickname came from her cheerful personality. Wherever Joy went, whether in work or play, she cast forth a bright spirit. Her happiness was so contagious that her life blessed many people.

Suddenly, Joy's life was deflated. First, her husband lost his position with a firm where he had been working for several years. Next, the shock threw him into a severe depression, leaving Joy with a sick husband and in a financial bind. These troubles took their toll on Joy's life; her joy drained out; her feelings changed drastically.

Then, something happened which Joy never dreamed would happen; she started having thoughts of harming herself. When the thought of suicide first came into her mind, she dismissed it as a once-in-a-lifetime thought. Later, when she had the thought again, she became frightened. Realizing that she was letting her problems overcome her, she knew that she must find help.

Then one night, while having her devotions, she found a note which she had written in her Bible: "God's promises are bigger than our problems." As she sat thinking about the meaning of this sentence, she asked herself: "Why not test this statement?" At this point Joy's devotion took on real meaning as she found many promises which spoke to her need. Because these promises spoke a message of assurance and hope, she claimed them to regain her emotional stability—her joy. God's promises focused the picture to let her see more than present circumstances.

Of course, Joy needed someone to help her unravel the parts of her life which caused her to have suicidal thoughts while under pressure. Nevertheless, her experience tells us there is something a person can do when bothered by thoughts of suicide. No person has to surrender to despair; there is help for hopeless people. A suicidal person can do something for himself.

God's promises *are* bigger than our problems. Regardless of the form, or source of a troubled Christian's problem, he can find and make a list of Bible promises. These promises will help clarify his distorted thinking, and remind him of the blessings in his life. They will put his burdens in proper perspective to uncover God's blessings.

Every person is responsible for staying alive. Therefore, a person having thoughts of suicide ought to accept responsibility for his life, not his death. This suggestion is a new attitude, the opposite of suicide. When one attempts to kill himself, he is accepting responsibility for his death. I am suggesting that anyone considering suicide should attempt to stay alive and accept responsibility for his life. I suggest that he stop feeling sorry for himself and get in the driver's seat. For after all, others can help keep a suicidal person alive, but he alone has responsibility for his life.

Still, acceptance of responsibility for one's own life is not an easy undertaking. When one takes this giant step, he will need someone trained in working with suicide to walk along beside as he or she moves from self-pity to self-direction.

If a suicidal person accepts responsibility for staying alive, what must he do to keep his life and avoid death? It is important that every such person know he can do something; and, he should begin immediately. He, and he alone, can take immediate action to stay alive.

HE CAN SOUND A CLEAR CALL FOR HELP

When a person accepts responsibility for his life, not his death, he will make certain that someone knows that he is in trouble, and needs help to stay alive. This is no time for subtle cries for help; others need to be aware of his struggle. They will not know unless he tells them in a language they understand.

A call for help is sometimes misunderstood. So it was

with Howard when he called his neighbor to help him move a piece of furniture out the door. After they tried without success, Howard said: "We may as well stop trying, because we will never get it out." "Get it out," exclaimed the neighbor; "I thought you were trying to get the cabinet into the house." All the time, the call for help was not understood; the man was pushing against him. Howard did not make a clear call for help.

If bothered by thoughts of suicide, one ought to give convincing cries for help. Many people in suicide crises make a serious error in judgment when crying for help. For some reason, friends, associates, and relatives fail to hear distress signals of people in suicide crises. When a suicidal person says, "I would be better off dead," the people who hear him often fail to hear the suicide clue. When one in a suicide crisis tells people, "You won't be seeing me around," they seldom hear or heed the warning. If one wants people to get the suicide message, he had better sound a clear call for help.

HE CAN GET PROFESSIONAL HELP

When a person accepts responsibility for his life, not his death, he ought to seek professional help immediately. Then while under the care of a psychologist or psychiatrist, he should cooperate with the treatment. The treatment will, of course, vary from person to person according to the philosophy and training of the counselor. However, regardless of the philosophy of the counselor and the treatment plan which he uses, several suggestions are indicated for most any suicidal person while in treatment.

■ *One should tell his therapist everything.* Most of us, especially when dejected, usually keep our weaknesses to ourselves. Many times this effort to keep our secret faults from other people spills over into our relationships with counselors. When this happens to a troubled person, he is cut off from needed help.

Psychiatrists and psychologists are trained to understand people; they are not mind readers. The counselor will not understand the person's problem if the person remains silent, denies that he has a problem, or avoids talking about his problem. One must *tell* his therapist what he is thinking and how he is feeling. For after all, who knows the content of one's mind, the effect of his early environment, and the unpleasant or shocking incidents of his life as well as the patient himself? In spite of the pain and complexity of the effort, if one will open up his life, a good counselor can help him deal with his struggle.

■ *One should follow the therapist's suggestions.* A psychiatrist once referred a couple to me for marriage counseling while he treated the husband separately for a psychotic problem. I was making progress with the couple, until late one night, I received an alarming call from the husband. When I answered his call, he announced that he had just slapped his wife down. I asked him why and got this response: "My psychiatrist told me that was what she needed." I told him he had called the wrong person; he needed to talk with the psychiatrist who was treating him.

This sick man had, of course, misinterpreted his counselor. This problem sometimes exists with mentally ill people; it can also be a problem when working with suicidal people. Thus, those who work with people struggling with suicide, usually give plain, specific instructions to the person.

These instructions are for a purpose; and the success of one's treatment may depend on how well he follows the directions. For instance, a psychologist or psychiatrist has no way, other than the protection built into his directives, to protect a person against self-harm. He cannot remain with a person twenty-four hours a day; his instructions can be one's constant companion.

■ *One should take prescribed medication according to directions.* Many people do not follow the directions for taking their medicine. One woman, so the story goes, phoned her doctor to ask if she should submerge her whole body in water while taking her prescribed medication. When her doctor did not understand what she was talking about, she explained: "The directions on the bottle say to take three times a day in water; does this mean that all my body needs to be covered with water when I take it?"

For best results and a safeguard, medication must be taken as prescribed. Also the patient should get a relative or friend to help him monitor his use of the medicine. Usually it is better for someone other than the suicidal person to administer drugs, as problems usually arise from misuse of medication. Failure in following the instructions for taking medication may have serious consequences.

■ *One should ask for an open phone help line.* Some psychologists and psychiatrists make an open-line agreement with suicidal people. For instance, the patient calls his therapist at specified times. If this cannot be arranged, he should have a trusted friend whom he can call in case of emergency; such an arrangement would be an emotional safety valve.

■ *One should seek to determine his real desire—to die or be rescued.* If bothered by thoughts of suicide, a person can get help for his ambivalent feelings that both cause him to want to escape life but also to want someone to rescue him from death; he has two opposite feelings or desires at the same time.

Every person ought to know that frequently suicidal efforts are successful; all too often nobody comes to the rescue. If one plans his own death, he had better count on being dead. If a person wants to stay alive, regardless of his reason for wanting to stay alive, he had better get help with his conflicting feelings.

HE CAN REVISE HIS PHILOSOPHY OF LIFE

Perhaps someone may say, "Don't come down so hard on people who have a false philosophy of life." I am not coming down hard on them; I am just doing like the little boy who was accused of hurting a cat. When the boy's mother heard the cat crying out in pain, she looked out the door and saw her son standing on the cat's tail. She screamed out to the boy, "Stop pulling that cat's tail." The boy said, "I am not pulling his tail, Mother; I am just standing on his tail; the cat is doing the pulling."

When a person accepts responsibility for his life, not his death, he can help himself stay alive by correcting his false philosophy of life. He needs to learn the difference between death and nonexistence; death is not nonexistence. True, one can end his earthly life, which is temporary; but he cannot end his existence, which is permanent. Accordingly, when one jumps off a bridge, takes an overdose of drugs, shoots himself with a gun, hangs himself with a rope, or takes some other deadly action, he escapes his earthly life by killing his body; however, he does not escape existence because one cannot kill his spirit.

Every suicidal person should know that suicide is a choice between life and death, not life and nonexistence. If one requires biblical documentation of this statement, he may read the Bible for himself (Acts 7:59). So every person ought to know that he should not plan on "ending it all"; death is just the beginning.

A biblical philosophy of life emphasizes two spiritual truths: Life is endless; life is more than flesh and bones. Let the person who is bothered by suicidal thoughts revise his philosophy of life under the light of these two spiritual truths.

LIFE IS ENDLESS

A familiar saying of suicidal people reflects a philosophy which is the opposite of belief in an endless life: "I will take a gun and end my life." These words are based on a false philosophy, because, again, one cannot end his life. He can bring his earthly life to an end but cannot bring the core of his existence to an end. Not only is life apart from everything and everybody, but also it is forever. When talking about suicide, the truth of one's endless existence should be noted.

As to one's existence, God crowned His creation when he created a human. An important fact of one's biological separation is that his separate existence is permanent; he is a creature of time and eternity. Life is more than a span on earth; it is everlasting. God created a human, a separate creature, for two worlds; therefore, a person will be around for a long, long time. One's life does not end at death, nor is it submerged into some cosmic future existence.

Think, "the soul of man never dies!" One can end his physical life; he can't end his spiritual life. One can kill his body; he cannot kill his everlasting spirit! Hope is realized when one believes in an endless existence.

LIFE IS MORE THAN FLESH AND BONES

People who view life as consisting of only flesh and bones accept a false philosophy of life; they need to learn that a person is a spiritual being. Because suicide focuses on a person's physical being, it makes the implication that death of the body destroys the person. An important fact of one's separate existence is his spiritual being, which cries out for meaning, purpose, life, God! He is more than body and brain; he is a spiritual being also.

■ *Don't be intimidated by smart alecks.* "But," someone may say, "we ought to stick with a scientific approach to a human's separate existence." This statement reflects the influence in our society, which has caused Christians to feel backed into an awkward corner. We often become confused in our study of human nature, because of our fear of being considered out of step with the popular thinking of our time.

I ask a person who makes the above statement: "What do you mean by a scientific approach?" If he considers a scientific approach as a view of a human which sees him as matter, without an independent spirit, I consider his view as a false scientism. Many people view one's spirit as being the product of his physical being; consequently, according to this view, when the body is dead, the spirit is dead. This view of a human is contrary to a belief in immortality that sounds forth from human history. The view is certainly inconsistent with biblical teaching. It is also inconsistent with the beliefs of many outstanding scientists.

One who is bothered by thoughts of suicide, and considers a belief in the immortality of a person as "unscientific," would do himself a favor by reading some good books by Christians who are also scholars in scientific fields. One who believes that a person is more than flesh and bones need not apologize for his academic and scientific company.

I make this personal appeal to any person who is bothered by suicidal thoughts: Some new footprints of thought lead weary and confused people to naught in their fruitless search for life. Your eagerness to make a "scientific approach" to new ideas and areas of truth may cause you to be exposed to a peculiar tendency of our generation—sincere people stumble along weird highbrow paths with little recognition of the obvious.

■ *Use the brain God gave you.* Do some serious thinking for yourself. Don't let would-be scholars dim your spiritual vision by their vain, and possibly false, sophistries; their deceptively subtle reasoning will confuse you. Don't let would-be scientists divert your attention from the spiritual aspects of life to a dangerous scientism which denies the spiritual nature of a person. Refuse to have your sense of direction detoured by the conflicting cries of this confused generation. Why let the befuddling of others direct your thinking to a lopsided view of humanity? Refuse to let your intellectual pride deaden your sensitivity to the unseen, but real. Scorn those who deny, or ignore, the spiritual nature of a person and use it foolishly to question Christian truth. Be not a miserable slave to humbug remedies that are based only on a physical human view and are prescribed in vain for suicide pain. Beyond integration of personality and social adjustment is spiritual life.

The spirit of a person is the crown of his existence. One does not have to lower his thinking to the level of a nincompoop to appreciate his spiritual nature. If possible, be an intellectual giant; but along with your brains, also seek to become a spiritual giant. One realizes hope for the hopeless in a true philosophy of life.

■ *How about your spiritual diet?* Notwithstanding all the religious activity and organization of the present time, we are experiencing a spiritual famine in the world. A dangerous emphasis on the physical nature of a person to the neglect of his spiritual nature has created the assumption that one can meet human needs apart from God.

The outgrowth of this view are methods and programs that have great value for meeting some of a person's needs, but that fail to meet the needs of the total person—spiritual needs as well as physical needs. Two cars in every garage do not feed the spiritual nature of a person. A nice house is not necessarily a home. Nice clothes for outward appearance are fine, but do not give inward peace. Good schools for training the minds of our children are a worthwhile goal for our society, but not enough for the total needs of children; education without spiritual values leaves a void in young lives.

All human resources appear exhausted and people continue to have outstanding needs; and many experience emotional bankruptcy. A human is a separate existence with a spiritual nature that reaches above and beyond the world of matter in which he lives. Our world is now suffering the consequences of stifled spirits. This spiritual famine is conducive to despair and suicide. Many suffer hopeless despair because of a false philosophy of life.

■ *Our progress has neglected the total person.* Human efforts are saturated with futility; our generation could be called the age of disappointment. Programs for progress are weighed and found wanting, not because of slackness of promotion but because they are based on a false philosophy—that we can meet the total needs of people without God. Modern drugs have worked wonders for physical and mental health; people are living better and longer than in the past. Technology has given our generation conveniences for living that our forefathers never dreamed possible; one need look no farther than electronic achievements to document this statement. Scientific discoveries have exposed many of nature's secrets to excite the fancy and stimulate the curiosity of people. Prosperity has inflicted serious wounds on one of our great enemies, poverty, to give us a land of plenty. Our movement into exploration of space gives excitement and expectation.

Few among us desire to turn back the clock to "the good old days." None would be likely to denounce or belittle the methods and programs that have elevated us and made our world a better, even if not safer, place in which to live. But something is missing. Our programs, commendable though they be, neglect an important aspect of our nature—the spiritual. Our progress and improvement have reached into every area of our lives—every area except the most important, our relationship to our Creator.

This work we ought to have done and not left spiritual work undone. Modern drugs may temporarily lift the spirit, but only God can give us permanent peace. Nice clothes, high powered automobiles, spacious homes, electronic wonders, and exciting entertainment fail to fill the empty place in our lives. Glimpses into the secrets of nature do not compensate for rest in the "secret place of the most High." A walk on the moon does not fill the need for a walk with God. The fruits of prosperity cannot satisfy our hunger for the Eternal.

HE CAN ENDURE APARTNESS WITHOUT LONELINESS

One annoying problem for every person is that of loneliness. This is a generation of lonely hearts. One need look no farther than the classified section of newspapers to hear the cry of loneliness. There he will find a depiction of the aching void of lonely people. This typical ad illustrates the point: "Very lonely; would like to share my home with someone who is also lonely." One hears such cries of lonely pain over and over; no person is exempt from its clutches. Eventually, to some degree loneliness touches every one of us; but it tears the suicidal person apart.

Loneliness has a prominent place in every geographical section, in every race, in every age. Where there are people, there is loneliness; and where there is loneliness, there is a cry for help. The suicidal person's cry for help because of his lonely feeling is at the heart of his problem. He is not able to cope with the lonely feeling that results from his aloneness.

People involved in a suicidal struggle make such remarks as: "I feel so alone"/"I feel like I am cut off from everybody"/"This world is a lonely place"/"I cannot handle my life alone." A person with this feeling, bothered by suicidal thoughts, can overcome the pain of his aloneness.

I am not suggesting that a person can escape his biological and theological apartness; escape from this apartness would be escape from his humanity. God created a person to be separate from everybody and everything (Gen. 2:7). I am suggesting that one can overcome his assigned or acquired aloneness, and can overcome the pain and loneliness of his inherited apartness. Personal experience of this truth may mean the difference between a deadly act to escape life and a dignified commitment to enjoy life. When a suicidal person accepts responsibility for his life, not his death, he can experience apartness without loneliness. This is realized in two ways: relationship with self and relationship with God.

TRANSFORM LONELINESS TO SOLITUDE

Awareness of a separate existence, rather than causing loneliness, can result in the opposite, solitude. The word *solitaire* well illustrates this truth. A solitaire may mean a gem, a diamond set alone as in a valuable finger ring. On the other hand, it may mean a life lived like a solitaire card game, played by only one person. If one acquires solitude, he is like a valuable diamond set apart with meaning and purpose. If he chooses the opposite—loneliness—he will live his life in loneliness as illustrated by a solitaire card game.

Solitude is rooted in self-acceptance. If one is to experience solitude, he must accept himself. What is self-acceptance? Several aspects of life result in self-acceptance. At least two aspects of personality are important for our present discussion. Let us examine them one by one.

First, a person accepts himself by having a healthy identity as a separate person, a wholesome image of himself. Even though he sees himself as being apart from everything and everybody, he knows that he is a distinct person. He is fully aware of his separate existence, yet he views his separate existence as a plus, not a minus. Self-identity means that the person knows who he is; he is not a stranger to himself.

For a person to change his loneliness to solitude, he must first meet himself. He must get to know the real self; he must experience a true introduction to the person who looks back at him from his mirror, walks in his shoes, sleeps in his bed, and sits in his chair. This relationship with one's self gives to him identity as a separate person. One reason that suicidal people are lonely is that they are strangers to themselves.

Not only does the person with a wholesome self-image know himself, he accepts himself. Lonely suicidal people are ill at ease with themselves. Perhaps someone will say, "But I can't stand myself." If one can't stand himself, he may need to straighten out his life. He may need to get his act together; he may need to master his own life.

Every person needs to meet the challenge of life by daring to be a distinct person with dignity. God intended for a person to be himself. One cannot escape his life; he should meet and master it. One cannot run away from his loneliness, because he cannot run away from himself. Consequently, if one is to overcome his loneliness, he must change it to solitude. By meeting and mastering his separate life, he can become the kind of person he can live with and enjoy. Such a person is alone, but not lonely.

Myself

I have to live with myself and so
I want to be fit for myself to know.
I want to be able as days go by
Always to look myself in the eye.
I don't want to stand, with the setting sun,
And hate myself for the things I've done.
I want to go out with my head erect;
I want to deserve all men's respect;
But here in the struggle for fame and pelf,
I want to be able to like myself.
I don't want to look at myself and know
That I'm bluster and bluff and empty show.
I can never hide myself from me;
I see what others may never see.
I know what others may never know.
I can never fool myself and so,
Whatever happens I want to be
Self-respecting and conscience free.

(© 1934, Edgar A. Guest)

Second, a person accepts himself by accepting the dignity and worth of himself, the worth and dignity of his unchangeable apartness. He knows that he is separate from everything and everybody, but he also knows that this apartness gives meaning to his life. The apartness that causes one to be lonely is also the distinction and value of his person. This dignity and worth make him important in the sight of his Creator, a unique person.

One's apartness from others and the world around him makes him unique. It enables him to stand off and observe others and the world, and it lets him interact with the "not-him." One's dignity is that he is a thinker, a knower, an actor. True, one is acted upon by stimulation from others and his world; yet his unique existence gives him the power to act upon others and the world. Thus the dignity and worth of his separate existence helps him overcome his loneliness. This dignity and glory of his life can change his lonely feeling to solitude.

God created man from the dust of the earth; man then became a living soul (Gen. 2:7). Every person is created in the image of God; he is important (Gen. 1:27). Reader, always remember that you are somebody; you are important; you are created in the likeness of God.

When I was a little boy, money in my home was scarce. Therefore when I found a coin in the dirt one day, I picked it up. The piece of money had been lost so long that its identity was concealed beneath the cankerous rust that covered it. Carefully I cleaned and polished the coin until an image became visible on its face. Finally I established its identity; I knew what it was because the image of a President was imprinted on it. The coin's worth was then established; it was no longer a nameless piece of metal.

So it is with a Christian: God has cleansed him and established his identity. The image of God is stamped upon his life. He is not just a nameless chunk of matter and spirit, lost in the sands of time. He knows who he is, and is able to live with himself. He has been claimed by the Lord; consequently, he lays claim to his own life. He has been found; therefore he has found himself. He is important, a child of God. He knows himself, and accepts himself. His loneliness has changed to solitude.

Solitude is rooted in the purpose of God. Solitude is grounded in the realization that God created humans for a purpose. One should accept and love himself in the fulfillment of that purpose. This love for one's self is not selfishness and pride that results in rebellion against God; neither is it a feeling of superiority toward others that results in a bad spirit. Let one love himself according to Bible teaching. The Bible commands us to love our neighbors as we love ourselves (Matt. 22:39).

This wonderful truth removes the feeling that one is cut off from life. It replaces this lonely feeling with a feeling of being at home in the universe. When one feels at home with his world, his inlook and outlook are different. The inner peace with himself results in a rewarding relationship with others. It thus changes his loneliness to solitude.

TRANSFORM LONELINESS TO FELLOWSHIP

■ *A relationship with the Lord resolves the conflict in a person's basic nature.* Divine help for overcoming human aloneness is at the very core of human survival and need. This help reaches to the root of one's problem of aloneness; it gives help beyond human help. As mentioned previously, one cannot escape his inherited apartness; however, he can open up his life to the presence of God and experience a transformation of that apartness. One cannot escape from his inherited aloneness, but he can have a guest, the presence of the Lord.

In past years preachers emphasized an important truth about the presence of the Lord. They proclaimed that the latch on the door to a person's inner life is on the inside; each person must open the door for the Lord to come into his life. To receive His presence, a person struggling with suicide must open the door. A person bothered by suicidal thoughts needs to know that God loves him and will enter his aloneness. When Jesus Christ enters a person's life, there is meaning and purpose for his survival. There is hope for the hopeless.

God wants every person to experience life, not a living death. Thus divine help goes to the very heart of the suicide problem; for the crucial issue for a person struggling with suicide thoughts is the strands of death in his aloneness. He wants life but life is too much for him to bear. God has given the answer; He has paid the price; He has resolved the problem. Jesus Christ gave the answer in very simple language: "I am come that they might have life, and that they might have it more abundantly" (John 10:10).

■ *This relationship is biblical.* The proposed answer does not avoid or reject the basic doctrines of the Bible. Rather, it views these doctrines as vital to the answer. For the doctrines of the birth, death, and resurrection of Jesus Christ explain this answer to aloneness. However, not the explanations, but the fact of His birth, death, and resurrection is the answer.

We need no longer live alone in the loneliness of our apartness. The central message of Christianity is that God, in the person of Jesus Christ, entered into our apartness to make a conquest for us that we could not make for ourselves. In the mysterious incarnation of Christ, God in truth came to be with us; God entered our aloneness.

The real meaning of the birth, death, and resurrection of Christ is that He won a victory in relationship. Jesus, both divine and human, conquered the loneliness and alienation of humanity. In a miracle beyond human comprehension, the divine and human were fused to achieve the redemptive accomplishment of God for us. When Christ died on the cross, not only were our sins paid for, but He also broke down the wall of partition. Christ lives to offer eternal reconciliation and release for the lonely and estranged sons of men.

■ *This relationship gives fulfillment of one's being.* Salvation is not one in which a person loses himself, but one in which he finds himself, becoming a child of God. The threat of aloneness is removed by the newly found identity and meaning for his life. Because of God's achievement in humanity, God in the person of Christ can now stand ready to enter any person's aloneness. Christ, both divine and human, is able to enter a person's fixed apartness.

Yet there are two important facts that we must remember: The redemptive work of God does not lessen one's existence; one's existence is not threatened but rather finds meaning, purpose, and fellowship in God and God in him. Neither does this salvation destroy one's freedom. One can exercise his freedom of will to remain in his aloneness, or to experience deliverance from it. This verse from the Bible conveys God's answer to one's aloneness:

> Behold, I stand at the door and knock; if any man hear My voice, and open the door, I will come in to him, and will sup with him and he with Me (Rev. 3:20).

A sweet story of a little girl at school gives an excellent illustration of loneliness transformed to fellowship. Three children who lived near the school had permission from their parents to stay after school and help the teacher. The little girls had a wonderful time helping their teacher with her work. Their chatter and giggles brightened the schoolroom.

Finally, their work was finished and they were ready to leave. So they told the teacher good-bye and left the building to go home. They had only a short distance to walk to their homes.

While finishing her work and thinking about the happy girls, the teacher heard the door of her room open. She looked up from her work and saw that one of the little girls had returned. When she saw that the girl was crying, she asked: "Honey, what is wrong?" The little girl answered: "I am afraid to walk home by myself; I feel lonely when I walk home alone." The teacher told her: "Go play outside and I will take you home in a few minutes."

Shortly the little girl came running into the room with a happy smile on her face and said: "I am not afraid to walk home now. My father has come to walk with me. I don't feel lonely when my father walks with me."

This story ought to be the story of our lives. Our lives involve us in uncertain, and sometimes frightening, possibilities. We, as the little girl, feel lonely and frightened by the unseen and unknown. Then our loneliness disappears as we joyfully move into the presence of Christ for our journey home. The words "I don't feel lonely and scared when Jesus walks with me" should ring from our lips and hearts.

Shortly after I became a Christian, an older couple helped me understand this precious truth. Being a young Christian with a desire to share my new life with others, I often visited this couple. My visits to this little home back in the woods enriched my life, and many pleasant visits are stored in my memory.

This man and woman had poor health and little contact with people. Yet their lives radiated a clear testimony of the Lord's presence. While they had limited outside contact, and had little Christian fellowship, they were not overcome with loneliness. The presence of Christ was real to them.

Years have passed since these lovely Christians went to be with the Lord. And much of what they said to a young Christian has been forgotten. Nevertheless, a mild rebuke has not been forgotten. When I casually mentioned one day that they lived way back in the woods alone, they responded, "Young man, we do not live alone; Jesus is always with us!" Their loneliness had changed to fellowship with Jesus Christ.

RESPONSIBILITY CAN STOP SUICIDE

One suicidal person expressed his unworthy and helpless condition with these words: "My life is a mess; I am no good. I have failed in everything. I am in the way; my family would be better off without me. I have no choice; my life is unbearable; I will end it all."

Another person once said, "My life is like Humpty-Dumpty." He then quoted a rhyme which he learned while he was a boy in school:

> Humpty-Dumpty sat on a wall.
> Humpty-Dumpty had a great fall.
> All the king's horses
> And all the king's men,
> Could not put Humpty-Dumpty
> Back together again.

The man said that his schoolbook also had a picture on the page next to the rhyme. The picture depicted an egg, shattered in a hundred pieces. This man felt that his situation was similar to the situation experienced by Humpty-Dumpty. He felt as though his life was shattered beyond repair; he considered himself beyond help. Finally, this man came to realize that his situation was different from that of Humpty-Dumpty.

When a person accepts responsibility for his life, not his death, he can realize change without suicide. A suicidal person wants things to be different; but because of his despair he sees no way of making things different, other than suicide. Suicidal people often say, "My life is so hopeless; I will kill myself and make things be different." There is good news; there can be change without suicide. One does not have to end his earthly life to bring about change in his life. For people who view suicide as the only way to change their lives, I suggest other ways to make life different.

A person who takes the first giant step from self-pity to self-direction has heard an important message of life. The message is simple but dynamic—life can change. A person in a suicide struggle needs to hear and heed this message. Because a suicidal person perceives his condition as remaining as it is, or even getting worse.

The announcement of this message is welcome news to a person who is on the road to despair; for one who has already reached such a state of despair, and is experiencing a suicide crisis, this news could be an important anchor for survival. A person in the anguish of a battle between life and death, needs to hear that life can change. There is hope for hopeless people.

FIRST, ONE CAN CHANGE ALONENESS.

If a person commits himself to staying alive, he may be able to change his aloneness. Someone, in what appears to be hopeless despair, may ask, "What can I do about my aloneness?" I have given response to this question in earlier discussions; but because of the nature and importance of this question, I repeat the response: If one means biological aloneness, the answer is, nothing; one is stuck with his separate existence. Escape would be liberation from his humanity; one cannot escape himself. If one is talking about assigned or acquired aloneness, he may be able to do something about it.

And if one's aloneness is a problem for him and he can do something about it, he would do well to focus his energy and time on making the change. Hear this, one can do more than he thinks he can do about his life. At an early age, I learned that I could do more than I thought possible to change my acquired aloneness.

Alone in the bottom of a fifty-foot well; how would he ever get out? Many such questions raced through the mind of the frightened twelve-year-old boy. It had begun several weeks before when a well-digger came to dig an open well on our place. My parents agreed for me to help the man dig the well. And, of course, I was enthusiastic about the new venture.

On this particular day my family was leaving to be away for the day. Before they left, I had them lower me into the new well so that I could dig until the well-digger arrived. My brothers let me down with the bucket that we were using to lift the dirt out of the well.

I immediately started work, expecting that the man would come in a short time. An hour went by and he did not come. Then, two hours, and finally three hours had gone by, and the well-digger had not come to work. My situation appeared hopeless. I had never felt so alone in all my life. Fifty feet below the surface of the earth in a four-foot square hole, I felt cut off from the whole world. Frightened, alone, and nobody within several miles, I was in the midst of a traumatic experience.

I learned two important lessons that day. I learned the awful pain of aloneness, and found the ability to change the circumstances that intensified it. I climbed fifty feet on the rope to the top of the well. When experiencing assigned or acquired aloneness, a person can do more than he thinks he can.

Many times people feel alone and afraid but believe that nothing can be done to change the situation. Also, there are those who feel overcome by their aloneness. People who work with troubled, suicide-inclined people often hear such despairing remarks as, "I feel so hopeless." One may feel that life cannot change. Perhaps he feels as though he is caught in the jaws of a vise. He may even feel that his life is in the grip of blind fate.

As already stated, even though a person cannot change his inherited separation, this should not keep him from trying to change his acquired separation. It is possible that one's life can be different. One may be able to escape his aloneness. When a person has enough motivation, the seemingly impossible often happens.

SECOND, ONE CAN CHANGE HIS THINKING AND FEELINGS.

Many suicidal people feel extremely unworthy, and feel helpless to do anything about these feelings. While trying to live their lives they have experienced one failure after another. Human frailty has overcome them. Because of low self-esteem, many of them feel unworthy of life. Death appears to be the only help for them. They see a forced choice—a miserable life or a suicide death. If a person who is bothered by suicide thoughts is willing to assume responsibility for his life, he need not kill himself to change his life. He can begin his responsible action by applying two questions to his life. I discuss these questions because of the importance of feeling and thinking in suicide.

Here is the first question: How does a person who is bothered by suicide thoughts begin his day? One so bothered should consider this: Early morning feelings, thinking, and acting usually set the direction of one's day. So to begin his day on a positive note, he will need to gain some control over this threesome.

While the three are so closely related they cannot be completely separated, some understanding and control is possible. One is not, as some believe, a slave to his unconscious with no control over his thinking, feelings, and behavior. True, the whole matter is very complicated. One's feelings certainly influence thinking and acting; so do thinking and acting each influence the other two members of the threesome.

But to be more specific for a positive beginning of one's day, consider the thinking that begins a day. Does one feed his mind the burned-out leftovers from the day before, or let depressing news invade his mental processes to ruin his day, or spend his early hours thinking of family conflicts or probable problems of the day? If so, he will probably be defeated before his day hardly begins.

A dejected person can change his early morning thinking. He can cultivate constructive thinking and change destructive thinking. He can fill his mind with thoughts that result in a creative and productive day. He can start the day with a song; Dr. Donald Gray Barnhouse used to tell how he and his wife made a habit of beginning each day singing the grand old tune, "May Jesus Christ Be Praised."

Negative thinking will take the pleasure out of one's day and bring him to its close feeling tired and unhappy. Let the person bothered with suicidal thoughts avoid low level thinking; let him scale the heights of high-level thinking. He can change his thinking and change his day, for how one starts out determines to some degree how he ends up.

Another question: How do suicidal people end their day? Many bring home the problems, the conflicts, and hurts from work to keep them company. Others end their day being consumed by unrealized goals, hatred, or jealousy. An increasing number deaden their thinking, feelings, and acting with alcohol or use of other drugs. Many, far too many, take on the problems of the world for an evening of morbid thinking.

Notwithstanding the nature of one's day, the suicidal individual should seek to end it in peace and relaxation. A morbid examination of one's day should be avoided; this approach would likely cause depression. A better approach is to recognize the unpleasant but dwell on the pleasant. If there are errors in a person's day that he can correct, let him do so immediately. He should not sweep the unpleasant under a mental rug to cause trouble later. Let one learn from the day's mistakes rather than becoming a slave to them. Let one rid his mind of bitterness and resentment to prevent their cancerous attack on him.

Let one tie up the loose ends of his day, for otherwise they will disturb his sleep and face him tomorrow. One should close out the issues and decisions of today and let tomorrow's issues rest while he rests. One should discover and enjoy the precious moments of his evening hours, rather than permitting hostility, envy, or discouragement to rob him of a pleasant evening. One dark recurring thought can blind one to the richness of the present moment. Some trivial and insignificant matter can blot out the beauty of one's environment, the preciousness of his loved ones, and the hopes of the future.

One morning I looked out across the hills at the beautiful scenery. It was a wonderful morning; there was so much beauty to see. Suddenly I decided to play a trick on myself. I reached into my pocket and pulled out two pennies, and then placed them in front of my eyes. This behavior made a drastic change in my life; all the beauty was gone. Two little insignificant pennies blotted out the beauty of life. So it is with many people: Life is beautiful until some trivial or insignificant matter blots out the beauty. A person should claim the enjoyment of every evening fragrance. It is now his; tomorrow it may be gone forever.

This approach is a tough assignment, but it is surely better than suicide. Granted, one will not be able to master all of these suggestions; however, he can gain some control over his thinking, feeling, and acting; and this contrast between positive and negative thinking reflects the contrast between dejection and happiness. Notwithstanding that one will need the help of someone for changing his thinking, with help he can do it. By so doing he will accept responsibility for his life, rather than responsibility for his death.

THIRD, ONE CAN CHANGE THE PAST.

Don't walk alone. A person can experience change in his life without suicide by settling his past. To deal with his past in a constructive manner he will need human and divine help. The human help must include someone trained to work with people who have suicidal problems. This person will walk with one as he empties the mental and emotional poison from his life. He will neither condemn nor condone the person's past; his work will be to support him as he settles the old accounts. One will be able to trust this professional person to deal with any past experience which may be causing his present trouble. Also, because the counselor accepts the person just as he is, the patient's opinions about himself change.

Don't be a prisoner of your past. Divine help for dealing with a person's past is on a different level, one that is spiritual. If one is a Christian, the Lord will also walk with him in dealing with his past. Howbeit, the main help from the Lord in dealing with the past is in setting one free from its bondage. Ghosts of the past move into the present to haunt many suicidal people, but the power of God is able to break the shackles of bondage to set them free.

In this relationship a person changes the past by submission of his life to the life-changing power of God. One does not have to die to escape his miserable life; beyond the help of man is the help of God. His life-changing power will give a renewal of one's mind, a cleansing of one's spirit, a direction of one's behavior.

One's greatest enemy is his unbelief. If an adult or a teenager can only trust Jesus Christ to change his life, his life can experience a miracle of grace. All things are possible, only believe! Listen to His invitation: "Come unto Me, all ye that labor and are heavy laden, and I will give you rest" (Matt. 11:28). There is hope for the hopeless in Jesus Christ; one may know change without death.

FOURTH, ONE CAN CHANGE HOPELESSNESS TO HAPPINESS

The writer of Ecclesiastes—probably Solomon—got caught in the struggle of life in his search for happiness. He did not like his life and wanted it to be different. In his unhappiness he put into his analysis of life the feelings of many who lived before and after him: What is there in life that will satisfy the longings of man's innermost being to make him happy. How can one find the good in life that will make life precious to him? What does human existence have to offer for permanent enjoyment? Such questions motivated this writer of old to carefully observe life. And Solomon was well equipped for his task, having great wisdom, authority, power, and wealth. He put life on trial. Consider what he learned.

■ *A happy life consists of more than knowledge.* Solomon first expended his energy in the acquisition of knowledge. He traversed the whole field of learning and reached the limits of human thought. His fair trial of knowledge convinced him that learning, by itself, could not deal adequately with life, sickness, sorrow, and death. He found from living that all his knowledge could not quiet the raging storm in his own life. He felt that his accumulated learning, if it be the only value in life, would end at death. His research revealed that knowledge, as a supreme value, was not enough to give meaning and happiness to life.

■ *A happy life consists of more than pleasure and delight.* Another area for Solomon's research with human life in a quest for happiness was sensual enjoyment. He centered his efforts on the pleasure and delight derived from excitement of his senses. He involved himself in everything that would satisfy his natural desires. He would try to find happiness by surrendering himself to his appetites.

This investigator concluded that self-gratification failed to meet the deeper needs of man to give happiness. He found that when he gave his life over to the excitement of his senses, he experienced delight for a short time only and then was left with an aching void, an empty feeling—unhappiness. Solomon also discovered that his desires were gaining control of his life, to make him a slave to that which offered no enduring happiness. It was not until his mind became dull and his whole organism exhausted that he realized that this was not the answer to the quest for happiness. When the vitality of life was gone, miserable and unhappy, he was left spent from his wild fling with destiny.

■ *Happiness consists of more than achievement and wealth.* Solomon then set out to find meaning and happiness for his life by human achievement and accumulation of wealth. But the emptiness and dejection remained in his life. Then too he realized that when death came, he would have to leave it all to others. Wealth and achievement were not the answer to his need for happiness.

■ *Happiness is a result of personal choice; every person chooses either hopelessness or happiness.* The writer of Ecclesiastes then came to a final conclusion as a result of his research on happiness. He did not discredit knowledge, or satisfaction of man's sensual needs, or accumulation of wealth and achievement, but he found that man could not give his whole life to any one, or all of these, and find the answer to the riddle of life; they failed to give true happiness. Apart from God's plan for life, Solomon found no answer. There is "nothing under the sun" apart from God that can fill the aching void of human existence. Man finds himself only when he finds himself in God. The Preacher, as he is called in the *King James Version*, gives a beautiful example of making the right choice. Rather than choose despair and death, he chose God.

Every human, to a greater or lesser degree, engages in similar exploration to that of the writer of Ecclesiastes. Life invites us to happiness. The choice is ours to make; we choose either happiness or hopelessness. Many choose hopelessness, to a degree that permits human survival, while they stew in their own misery. Not so with the person in a suicide crisis; he has followed a hopeless path to the point of despair.

SUMMARY

A small boy went with his parents to the bank to withdraw all their money to purchase a vacation cottage. As the parents traveled back to their home, they discussed the amount of money they had for the purchase. The father said, "If we had $10,000 more, we could buy a better cottage." The little boy finally got his father's attention, and said, "Daddy, if you had put more in the bank, you would have got more out."

This boy's advice is good advice for a suicidal person. If one puts more into life, he will get more out of life. What then can a person do when he is bothered by thoughts of harming himself? He can take responsibility for his life, rather than his death. When he makes such a commitment, the promise of hope for the hopeless is fulfilled. Earthly life continues, because death is swallowed up in hope; and hope blossoms out in life!

9 HOW HOPE FOR THE HOPELESS CAN BE REALIZED

It was a breathtaking experience for a group of teenagers. The two-hour pool party was now coming to an exciting end. The excitement came from the enchanting moon, so bright and beautiful. During the closing moments of the party, the young people stood gazing up at it in silence; they found no adequate words to describe its beauty. The night was one of those rare occasions when life bubbles over the thrill of being alive. This pool party had special meaning for these young people because they were Christians who enjoyed having clean fun together.

The Sunday School teacher broke the silence by reminding the young people that it was time for the party to end. "Good night; see you in Sunday School on Sunday," filled the air as the teenagers walked to their automobiles to leave. In the meantime Albert, the host of the Sunday School party, walked slowly along the edge of the pool toward his house.

"Look, look!" Albert suddenly shouted, pointing to the pool. The others rushed back to the pool, thinking someone had drowned in the pool. But what they saw was not a body but a brilliant reflection of the moon. The young people gazed in awe, first at the moon in the heavens, and then at the moon in the pool.

Albert, wanting to have some fun, said: "Watch me shatter the moon." So saying, he threw a rock into the pool, breaking the moon into a thousand pieces. Everybody shouted, "Albert, you villain, you have shattered the beautiful moon."

At this point the teacher walked up to the pool. "See the beautiful moon shining in the heavens; you cannot shatter it; and soon it will put the moon in the pool together again." By this time the ripples in the pool had settled, enabling the pool again to reflect the moon.

As the young people again enjoyed the beautiful moon in the heavens and the beautiful moon in the pool, the teacher closed the party with a spiritual truth: "Sometimes the rocks of life shatter our lives; life falls apart. However, God is not shattered; His love continues to shine upon us. When the ripples of life are settled, He restructures our lives to make them beautiful again. As Albert caused the water not to be receptive to the moon, sometimes our lives are so unsettled that they are not receptive to God's love and strength."

During these troublesome times when America is afflicted with a suicide epidemic, this Sunday School teacher's lesson needs to be considered. The beautiful reflection of life is often shattered by the rocks being thrown from every direction—the detrimental factors and forces around us. Nevertheless, we can learn some spiritual truths along with these teenagers: While the destructive forces of our world cannot shatter God, they can unsettle our lives to prevent them from being receptive to his love and help. Even God cannot help us if our lives shut Him out by the destructive forces which ripple through them. Therefore, it behooves us to deal with these destructive rocks; for by so doing, we make it possible for God's love to shine down into broken humanity and restructure our lives. Hope for the hopeless will be realized as we learn this spiritual truth.

Yet for this hope to be realized, we must accept and deal with several truths. As we respond to these truths in a positive way, hope for the hopeless masses will become reality. What then are these truths?

THE SUICIDE EPIDEMIC IS REAL

The suicide epidemic is a real issue of concern. It is not a problem at which we can blink our eyes to cause it to go away. It is not a myth, a figment of our imaginations. It is a hard cold reality of American life.

We can sum up the suicide problem in a fourfold conclusion: Every human being has a fixed apartness from everything and every person; most people handle their apartness to live their lives and rise to human dignity, while a few sink to human despair; while some people love life and want to hold on to it, others hate life and want to end it; life is determined by how we handle what happens to us rather than by what happens to us.

Because of the increase in the rate of Americans who hate their lives and want to destroy themselves, suicide has become a major problem. Therefore, we cannot afford to relegate suicide to a dark cellar of secrecy. We must bring it out in the open and deal with it. No longer can those who care about people act as though suicide is a problem for others. This challenge is especially ripe for Christian love and action; therefore, let us tune our ears to the cry for help, and focus our vision on souls in despair.

THE CHURCH SHOULD BEGIN TO BATTLE

The time has come for the church to enter the battle against the problems of our time. In the past, she has blazed the trail in giving motivation, programs, and procedures for dealing with current problems. What has happened to this spiritual initiative? The church needs no apology for her mission, message, or Master. Her mission continues to be a must for our generation; her message is by no means out-of-date; her Master continues to confront the needs of broken humanity to offer salvation and life.

Our churches must be strong to meet the challenge of the suicide epidemic. Yet one is appalled by the spiritual climate of many churches. The childish bickering and fighting in many churches is enough to make those weep who love the church, and desire the fulfillment of her mission. Most church trouble is caused by people who are either mentally sick, emotionally immature, or power hungry. If these people move into power, and many of them do, the result is tragedy, because the church fellowship is disturbed, the church program is paralyzed, and the church community left in spiritual darkness. These people should by no means be turned away from the church. They should be helped, but they should not be permitted to gain control of the church.

Programs and services for suicidal people, along with other church tasks, will become a reality when a majority of church members take the initiative in loyalty to Jesus Christ, and in service to the sin-sick, trouble-trapped, downtrodden members of the human race. A church cannot hope to mend broken lives if the life of the church itself is shattered. The ripples in a church prevent God's love from being reflected to troubled people.

Our churches must face the challenge of a sick society, including the suicide epidemic. Suicide is spreading across America in the fragile soil of our restless society. Conditions in our land are conducive to despair. Many people have much to live with, but little to live for; consequently, they turn to self-inflicted death.

I am not saying that everything is wrong with American life, because when one views the American scene, he sees much that is right in our country. We have a right to be proud of the many good things in our land; I am proud to be an American citizen; and I would not trade my citizenship with a person in any other country. Nevertheless, while I give thanks for the blessings of America, I must be realistic and face the problems of our society.

The work being done in suicide prevention by professionals, public agencies, and volunteer workers is of tremendous importance. Nevertheless, these contributions do not relieve the church of its opportunity and responsibility. The church has the mission, the message, and the fellowship to move to greater healing depth in suicide prevention and treatment. Hope for the hopeless masses of mankind will best be realized, if realized at all, when churches face their task in faith and love.

A church of the '80s must meet the compelling challenge of our time. The suicide epidemic is frightening; now is the time for action. Let churches arise to fill the gap between human potential and human despair. Movement of churches in meeting this challenge will be visible in two areas of church work: the teaching and preaching of great Bible doctrines will permeate the thinking of church members and will spill over to have an impact on society, and Christian workers will project and carry out programs to help suicidal people.

I am not suggesting that the main mission of a church is to prevent people from killing themselves. What I am saying is that when a church takes its mission seriously, the spiritual truths will be proclaimed with enough enthusiasm to influence people to live their lives without defeat and despair. When a church reaches this state, suicide prevention and suicide crises treatment will flow spontaneously into the suicide tragedy. Hope for the hopeless will be realized.

Our churches must be the love of God to suicidal people. A church is a unique fellowship of Christian people. If love, friendship, acceptance, and understanding are to be found anywhere, church should be the place. If any group can bring a person to a choice of life over death, and inspire him to find his place in life, the church ought to be that group. The very nature of a church should enable one to find both rest and unrest in her fellowship: rest from the struggles of life, but a restless urge toward living the abundant life. This is the basic need of the person who has an inclination toward suicide. Hope for the hopeless is to be found in the meaning, the message, and the mission of a New Testament church.

SUICIDE: EVERY CHRISTIAN'S CONCERN

While the church has a responsibility for meeting the challenge of the suicide epidemic, and every Christian ought to be concerned, life is the burden or blessing of each individual. Suicide is different from homicide, where one's life is in the hands of another person. One's life is his own, because hope for the hopeless flows into an important principle of life: It is not what happens to you, but how you respond to what happens to you that determines your life. I like the proverb: "It is not the direction of the wind, but the set of the sail that determines the sailing of the boat." Most people experience pressure and find some acceptable way of handling it. Others experience the same amount, or less, and kill themselves.

I had a dear friend when I was a young Christian who taught me this wonderful truth one afternoon. While this man experienced enough stress to move him into despair, he moved into inner peace and thanksgiving for life. This man spent eight years in his room except for a few weeks in a hospital. He was paralyzed from his neck down; yet God's grace had moved upon his afflicted life to raise him above his suffering.

As I approached his home for my visit with him, I was thinking this man likely spends many anxious moments. He was sick, helpless, and much of the time alone. My knock on the door got a response from the bedroom down the hall: "Come in." I entered his room, greeted him, and sat down in a chair by his bed.

While I sat listening to him talk, he interrupted himself saying, "Listen, listen. Look, look!" It took a few seconds for me to interpret what was happening. I then saw and heard a little bird chirping in a tree outside his bedroom window. He continued talking: "See that little bird in the tree singing? That little bird would not fall to the ground without God's knowing about it. Just think—He has told us that we are of more value than many sparrows. He is such a wonderful God; we can trust Him; He is so good to us."

This dear man expressed the opposite of despair. No, it was not denial of reality. It was not blind commitment to fate. It was active trust and commitment to the love of his Heavenly Father. This trust is the real answer to despair and suicide. It is this trust and commitment that Jesus is talking about in Matthew 6:24-34. He urges us to refuse to be pulled apart by anxiety. Rather, He asks us to trust the God who loves and keeps us by His love.